The
Hot & Spicy
Cookbook

MOIRA HODGSON

～～ T H E ～～

HOT & SPICY COOKBOOK

PRENTICE HALL PRESS

～～

New York   London   Toronto   Sydney   Tokyo

Prentice Hall Press
15 Columbus Circle
New York, New York 10023

Originally published in the United States by McGraw-Hill.

PRENTICE HALL PRESS and colophon are registered
trademarks of Simon & Schuster, Inc.

Library of Congress Cataloging-in-Publication Data
Hodgson, Moira.
    The hot & spicy cookbook / Moira Hodgson.
        p.   cm.
    Originally published: New York : McGraw-Hill, c1977.
    Includes index.
    ISBN 0-13-394784-X
    1. Cookery, International.   2. Spices.   I. Title.
TX725.A1H55   1989
641.6'383—dc20   89-3939
                                                          CIP

Designed by Patricia Fabricant
Manufactured in the United States of America

10   9   8   7   6   5   4   3   2   1

First Prentice Hall Press Edition

FOR MY PARENTS

My thanks go to the
Moroccan National Tourist Office and to
Hassan Esserghini, Mary Jarrett, Elizabeth Tingom,
Raeford Liles, and Bully.

CONTENTS

INTRODUCTION

It is hardly surprising that Americans have taken so readily to hot, spicy cooking. Food shops in ethnic neighborhoods, with their burlap bags of beans, jars and boxes of spices, dried chilies, exotic fruits and vegetables, dried and pickled fish, and piles of nuts and roots, are delightful places to whet the appetite and discover new ingredients. Abroad, the *souks* of Morocco, the open markets of Mexico, the bazaars of India and the Far East, all tempt even the most amateur of cooks. The warm, musky aroma of dried spices piled high in bins captures the imagination. Turmeric, tamarind, aniseed, mustard seed, cumin, bay leaves, pepper, cardamom, saffron—their vivid colors wait to be scooped up by the vendor and shoveled into newspaper cones, which are dropped into your shopping basket. Small boys hawk bunches of fresh coriander and mint, and the scent catches you as you pass and makes you ponder over fish, shrimp, or chicken. Then there are the chutneys, pickled lemons, glistening olives, peppers, oranges, tomatoes, and strings of onions—all these add to the fascination of spicy food.

Columbus' search for a spice route to the Indies led him to the continent of America, where he found the capsicum plant that yields the fiery little peppers that now appear in hundreds of varieties all over the world. To follow their journey is to trace the voyages of discovery and trade. This chapter is but a cursory glimpse into the cooking traditions that have developed around chili peppers, an indispensable feature of the goulashes, *sambals*, *satés*, and curries of these pages.

The biggest chili-eating region of the United States is the Southwest. Chilies are not only used in Mexican dishes, they are added to corn bread, potatoes, beans—even to spaghetti sauces. The food of this dry, rolling country is a combination of frontier cooking (barbecued ham, beef, sausages, spareribs, chicken, and steaks) and Mexican-Indian cooking, which is based on corn, beans, chilies, peppers, squash, and tomatoes. This "Tex-Mex" food is richer in meat and cheese than Mexican but features such Mexican specialties as *tamales* (steamed corn husks filled with corn dough and meat), *chiles rellenos* (large, spicy green chilies stuffed with cheese and fried in an egg batter), *chorizos* (hot sausages), and, of course, tortillas combined with different fillings and appearing as *enchiladas, tacos,* and *quesadillas.*

Chile con carne (chili with meat) is a Tex-Mex triumph. Its ingredients are as variable as the traditional stew. It is generally accepted, however, that the genuine version should contain beef cubes, dried chilies, oregano, and cumin simmered with a little water. Cornmeal is sometimes used to thicken the sauce. (Mexican *Chile Con Carne* is a thinner version, often made with meat other than beef.) One of the best Texan chilies I've had contained beer and bitter chocolate. The hamburger-chili-beans variety most often sold in cans is unacceptable to anyone who knows real chili.

In addition to beans, which are eaten throughout the Southwest (simmered with chilies and onions, sometimes mashed with scallions, peppers, and cumin, and tossed in oil and vinegar), chick-peas are a popular vegetable. They were brought to the continent by the Spanish. They can be mashed and baked in a soufflé; cooked with meat and chilies; or simmered with slices of *chorizo* and diced chili.

Mexican immigrants in California introduced turkey *mole poblano,* a holiday dish and one of the most remarkable inventions of Mexican cooking. The sauce is made from a combination of almonds, chilies, raisins, tomatoes, onions, garlic, sesame and pumpkin seeds, sugar, bread, tortillas, herbs, cinnamon, and cloves with bitter chocolate, all ground and simmered in stock until thick. The result is dark, spicy, and rich—you can't taste the chocolate but the sauce is not the same without it. There is a legend that it was invented by a group of nuns in the Santa Rosa Convent in Puebla. When the archbishop paid them a surprise visit they had nothing to offer him for dinner, so they prayed for inspiration and, guided by heaven, they went into the convent kitchen and ground or chopped all the edibles they had. Then they slaughtered the convent turkey and put it into the pot. The archbishop was, of course, delighted.

This famous story is probably apocryphal. According to Elisabeth Lambert Ortiz, an authority on Mexican food, *mole poblano* is typically Aztec. The Spaniards reported seeing clay pots filled with a rich dark sauce simmering in the marketplaces on their initial visit to Mexico. *Mole* powder is now available, but most Mexicans view it with scorn and prefer to grind their own spices.

Cuban and Puerto Rican immigrants have made an important contribution to American cooking. Frequently served specialties include black beans; fried plantains with pork cracklings; *ropa vieja* (literal translation: "old clothes"), shredded beef in a thick, reddish brown sauce; and *sofrito,* a rich garlicky tomato sauce, popular throughout the Caribbean and often used to flavor soups and stews. Cubans have also brought their own version of *arroz con pollo,* using chilies, olives, and capers where the Spanish used artichoke hearts, asparagus tips, and beans.

The Chinese settled in Cuba in great numbers and a fascinating new cuisine grew up. Those Cuban-Chinese immigrants who then came to the United States opened flourishing restaurants in New York and Florida. A typical meal may begin with black bean soup laced with rum. Subsequent courses may consist of fried rice, Chinese vegetables, fried plantains, and *picadillo*—chopped beef cooked with olives, raisins, tomatoes, and peppers. *Picadillo* was probably a Moorish dish brought over by the Spaniards, tomatoes and peppers being the Cuban contribution. Black beans and rice is another Cuban dish, which reveals its history in its name, *Moros y Cristianos* (Moors and Christians).

Immigrants from Hungary have also made an impact on American cooking. Hungarians invented the magical combination of lard, onions, and pure ground paprika that so impressed Escoffier that he introduced two Hungarian dishes into the *grande cuisine* of France: Hungarian goulash and chicken paprikash.

While Indians used the chili pepper whole and the Spaniards mixed it with spices, the Hungarians were the first to use their version of the chili pepper, a descendant of the American capsicum plant known as paprika, in powdered form unmixed with anything else. Hundreds of varieties of paprika peppers grow in Europe and they range from hot to sweet. In the Balkans, people grind the dried peppers and use them in stews or sauces, or slice them fresh and serve them with chopped onions in oil as a side dish. They also use paprika to spice sausages and ham.

Most of the major cities of the United States have excellent restaurants serving a cosmopolitan cuisine, but the town with the highest reputation for its food is New Orleans. Creole cuisine is a blend of Choctaw, French, Spanish, and African.

Miles of inland waterways teeming with crayfish and the long coastline with oysters, crabs, shrimp, and pompano make New Orleans especially good for seafood. The culinary term *creole* has come to mean a spicy concoction of tomatoes, green peppers, onions, and garlic. Cayenne and Tabasco peppers were brought north to the port of New Orleans by the Spaniards, along with spices from Latin America and the Caribbean. One of the most famous Louisiana specialties is gumbo (the name comes from the African word for okra), halfway between a soup and a stew. A highly seasoned *roux* is its basis—to which are added scallions, herbs, and a choice of either shellfish (oysters, crayfish, or shrimp) or meat (chicken, veal, or ham). The most important ingredient is filé powder, first used by the Choctaw, which is made from ground sassafras leaves and thyme.

One of the best meals I've ever had was along the River Road between New Orleans and Baton Rouge. I stopped for lunch on a cold, gray day at an unprepossessing little truck-stop café. There was no choice—you took what the proprietor served. I began with a steaming bowl of seafood gumbo and went on to large, succulent crayfish stuffed with herbs and spices in a light tomato sauce. The meal ended with wonderful black Louisiana coffee.

The Spanish conquistadores were astonished when they arrived in Tenochtitlán (now Mexico City) to find an extremely sophisticated Aztec cuisine. Bernardino de Sahagún, a Spanish priest who was there at the time, wrote of "white fish with yellow chili; gray fish with red chili; frogs with green chili; newt with yellow chili; lobster with red chili, tomato, and ground squash seed; white fish with a sauce of unripened plums; *tamales* made with honey . . ." Over a thousand dishes were served at the court of Montezuma and many of these have remained unchanged to this day. Tortillas, *tamales, tacos,* and *quesadillas*; dark, spicy sauces; and corn, beans, squash, pumpkin, peanuts, manioc, vanilla, cashews, cacao (the basis of chocolate), avocados, papaya, sweet potatoes, pineapple, and turkey were staples. The conquistadores introduced oil, wine, onions, garlic, chicken, cinnamon, cloves, rice, wheat, peaches, apricots, pigs, and cattle (and subsequently butter and milk).

Although Mexican food is often fried in lard, it is never greasy when properly cooked. Among the more interesting specialties are *huevos rancheros* (eggs fried and served with beans, chili sauce, and tortillas); *guacamole* (mashed avocado with tomatoes, onions, chilies, and lime juice, served with tortilla chips); and *pescado yucateco* (fish Yucatán style, cooked with pimientos, chilies, olives, and orange juice). When I was in Yucatán I ate shrimp cocktail almost every day. It was not the tired mixture of overcooked shrimp with bottled tomato sauce that often passes in restaurants, but an arrangement of very fresh, cold shrimp on a plate with chopped onion, tomatoes, chilies, and fresh coriander and an olive oil and lime-juice dressing.

At dusk in Chiapas, where I lived, in highland Maya country, the aroma of frying *quesadillas* would float up the hill. These are tortillas folded over a piece of cheese and fried until the outside is crisp and brown and the cheese is melted inside, which my neighbor would cook over a charcoal brazier and sell from her doorway to people in the street. She always spooned hot red *salsa* on top. Throughout Latin America *salsa* is as indispensable on the table as salt and pepper in other countries. It is often made from raw or cooked tomatoes, with peppers, spices, onions, and chilies, and used as a dipping sauce. The hottest table sauces are found in Yucatán.

Farther south, the long coastline of Central America yields an abundance of fish which is often cooked with tropical fruits and vegetables such as bananas, coconuts, oranges, limes, and lemons, combined with chilies.

South America is dominated by the Andes, which stretch for 400 miles from Venezuela almost to the foot of the continent, parallel to the Pacific Coast. The food is partly African, partly Moorish, and tropical, but most of all Indian—Aztec, Incan, and Mayan.

The potato was developed in Peru, where the Incas flourished until the Spaniards arrived. The Indians invented a method of drying potatoes by slicing them very thin and exposing them to the freezing mountain air day and night until the moisture evaporated. Ordinary potatoes are mashed with cream cheese, olive oil, and chilies (known in Peru as *ají*). *Ají* is related to the Mexican chili but it has a different flavor. Among outstanding Peruvian dishes are *ají de gallina* (chicken simmered in a spicy sauce made from chilies and walnuts) and *seviche* (fish, scallops, or shrimp marinated in lime or lemon juice with garlic, onion, and chilies). The fish turns white, "cooked" by the lemon juice. *Anticuchos,* a close cousin to the Indonesian *saté,* are a form of kabob made from beef heart cut into small cubes, threaded on skewers, and marinated in chilies, garlic, and orange juice. They are grilled over hot coals. I made them often in Mexico and served them with a sauce of coriander, raw onion, and orange juice. They are delicious—and very cheap.

A Bolivian specialty is *picante de pollo,* a hearty chicken stew made with garlic, onions, sweet peppers, thyme, marjoram, and *locato* (the local chili pepper). One-dish meals called *chupes* resemble the French *pot au feu* except that they contain substantial amounts of chili, which helps the Indians keep out the mountain cold.

Less chili is used in Colombia and Venezuela than in Peru and Bolivia, although the Spanish influence has given the food a piquant taste. *Pabellón* (spiced shredded beef) is similar to *ropa vieja* and is often served with fried plantains and rice. In Caracas you can get excellent beef grilled and served with a hot peppery table sauce; along the Venezuelan coast, fish is often cooked in coconut milk. Food in Chile, Argentina, and Uruguay is more European and generally not as spicy as it is in Mexico, Brazil, and parts of Central America.

Brazilian cooking has a totally different character than the rest of South American cooking. It is predominantly a mixture of Indian, Portuguese, and African ingredients. Manioc, a root crop, was the principal staple of the Indians. Corn, sweet potatoes, and peanuts were probably imported from other parts of Latin America; bananas, coconuts, yams, and okra were brought over by African slaves. The food has a distinctive yellow-orange color brought about by the use of dendê oil (palm oil), which is sold in varying shades from red to pale yellow all over Brazil. Malagueta pepper, from the east coast of Africa, is also used as a seasoning. The pepper actually originated in the Americas and was taken to Africa and brought back again. The most famous cooking in Brazil is Bahia, which shows a strong African influence. Fish and shrimp are cooked in dendê oil with nuts, ginger, and peppers or simmered in coconut milk. Hearts of palm is a popular salad (fresh hearts are *quite* different from canned); cassava meal is sprinkled over fish, meat, and poultry.

Like other Latins, Brazilians are fond of table sauces; in their version, called *môlho de pimenta,* both chilies and malagueta peppers are used. The country's national dish, *feijoada completa,* originated in Rio de Janeiro. Dried and smoked meats, including dried beef, tongue, fresh beef, pork, bacon, sausage, corned spareribs, and pig's feet are arranged on a platter and served with collard greens, cassava meal, sliced oranges, and *môlho de pimenta e limão,* a dipping sauce made from chilies and lemons.

The cooking of the Caribbean is extremely eclectic. The islands, colonized by the Spanish, French, Portuguese, Dutch, British, and Danish, frequently changed hands. But what gives Caribbean food its distinctive flavor is the use of indigenous island produce such as mango, guava, plantain, pineapple, coconut, breadfruit, cassava, and fresh seafood, including lobster, crayfish, conch, and shrimp.

The food is characterized by tomatoes and chili peppers, a taste that goes back to the original inhabitants, the Carib and Arawak Indians, who were using chilies probably brought over from Yucatán when the Spaniards first arrived. The Arawak also grew cassava, yams, sweet potatoes, corn, guava, cashews, and pineapples. They were hunters and lived on game and fish. Europeans brought oil, wine, vinegar, oranges, limes, lemons, rice, and coffee. During the years of the slave trade, between the mid-sixteenth and mid-nineteenth centuries, a totally different cuisine came into being. The Africans introduced okra, an important feature of the creole gumbo, and a penchant for spicy seasoning. Cinnamon, ginger, nutmeg, allspice, and cloves combined with chilies and peppers have become important components of Caribbean cooking. Meat is often marinated before it is cooked and simmered in a sauce containing chilies, onions, garlic, tomatoes, coriander, and thyme.

When the slaves were freed in the mid-nineteenth century, many of them preferred working in the sugarcane fields to remaining servants. There was a demand for new labor, which came this time from China and India. And so two more cuisines were introduced.

The Chinese brought their methods of cooking and growing vegetables; the Indians brought rice, curries, and chutneys. Most islanders use a curry powder that they mix themselves. Kabobs and pilafs are also now part of local cooking. A typical Caribbean table today might include kabobs, a curry, rice, and Chinese vegetables along with chutney, fried plantains, and grated fresh coconut.

In Guadaloupe I have eaten *poisson en blaff*, which is prepared with a mixture of French and island cooking techniques: red snapper is marinated in lime juice and chilies, then simmered in white wine with malagueta peppers and chilies. In Trinidad I have had conch curry and the smallest, sweetest oysters I have ever found anywhere served with a peppery sauce delicate enough not to mask their flavor. I also remember a spicy chicken soup in Aruba cooked with pumpkin, sweet potatoes, corn, beans, peas, and red peppers. It was just the thing after a long morning swim.

West African food is similar in many ways to Caribbean but it is generally "hotter." Dishes as colorful as the local handicrafts are cooked in orange dendê oil with tomatoes, red chilies, green peppers, and onions. Fish from the Atlantic Coast is plentiful. It may be fresh, dried, salted, or smoked. Peanuts are frequently used to thicken sauces—chicken is stewed in coconut milk with ground peanuts, garlic, onions, peppers, and tomatoes; shrimp is served in peanut sauce flavored with crushed chili peppers. Sauces are also thickened with mashed yams or a purée of black beans, potatoes, plantains, or grated coconut.

Africans are extremely inventive with yams, pounding them to a paste called *fufu* that is served with grilled meat and stews. They also make them into croquettes and chips, or mash them with crushed chili peppers or freshly grated nutmeg.

Meat in Africa usually has plenty of flavor but tends to be tough because most farm animals are free ranging. It is often marinated before being cooked. A popular marinade in Senegal is known as *yassa*. Lemon juice, chopped onions, chilies, salt, and pepper are mixed together and poured over the meat, which is left to stand in the mixture for a couple of hours.

Jollof rice, an African specialty much like paella, is eaten all over the continent. Meat or chicken is marinated in lemon juice with garlic, tomatoes, and onions, then browned and cooked with tomatoes, garlic, chilies, and ginger. The rice is stirred in and cooked at the end. *Jollof* rice is served with hard-boiled eggs, spinach, or cabbage.

A combination of African and Portuguese cooking has developed in Angola and Mozambique. Mint, cinnamon, cloves, saffron, coriander, cumin, and red peppers are popular aromatics. Shrimp is eaten frequently, cooked in olive oil and coconut milk with chilies, coriander, tomatoes, and onions. Chicken is stewed with cashew nuts and served with coconut rice.

Piri-piri, a fiery table sauce, is eaten with steak, lamb, chicken, fish, and shellfish. Tiny fresh red chilies are simmered in lemon juice, removed, and pounded to a paste. The sauce keeps well and is the African counterpart to *salsa*.

South African cooking is a curious mixture of Dutch and Southeast Asian. Moslem immigrant workers from Java, Sumatra, and Malaya have brought with them a cuisine similar to that of

Pakistan, introducing kabobs, curries, chutneys, *sambals, biryanis,* and *blatjangs.* They also brought a knack for pickling and preserving fish. Fish is sliced and fried in oil, then preserved in a mixture of chilies, turmeric, homemade curry powder, ginger, brown sugar, bay leaves, and wine vinegar. Other Moslem-inspired dishes include *bobodie,* a spicy mincemeat pie made with ground lamb seasoned with curry and lemon juice; and *sosaties,* cubes of lamb marinated in onions, curry powder, chilies, garlic, and tamarind water and cooked like the *shashlik* of the Middle East—skewered and roasted over an open fire with the marinade used as a sauce. *Bredie* is a South African goulash spiced with ginger, chilies, cinnamon, and cloves.

Farther north, Ethiopians are fond of a fiery seasoning called *berbere,* which is used on grilled or raw meat or as a flavoring in stews (known in Ethiopia as *wat*). Each cook has his own special way of preparing it. Red chili peppers are dried and pounded in a mortar. Ginger, garlic, and onions are ground with cloves, cinnamon, nutmeg, cardamom, allspice, fenugreek, peppercorns, and coriander.

North African food is less hot but very spicy. Cinnamon, cumin, saffron, turmeric, ginger, black pepper, cayenne, aniseed, paprika, and sesame seed are used in the food of the Maghreb people who live in Morocco, Algeria, and Tunisia. *Couscous* is the national dish of the Maghreb. A fine semolina, made from wheat grain, is steamed over a lamb or vegetable stew. Chick-peas, onions, carrots, zucchini, peppers, eggplant, leeks, raisins, and celery might be included in this stew. The vegetables are cut into large pieces and arranged at the bottom of a *couscoussière,* seasoned, and covered with water. The steam that rises from their simmering cooks the semolina, which is placed in a perforated pot over the top. *Couscous* can be served with *harissa,* a pungent pepper sauce that, when thinned with olive oil, is used with brochettes or served on olives or with salads. While Moroccan *couscous* is generally flavored with saffron, Algerians use tomato purée and the Tunisians make a very spicy sauce with chilies and ginger.

The last time I had *couscous* was something of a celebration. I was with friends in Marrakesh. We had noticed women (newlyweds) whose hands and feet were painted with henna—the result was like a beautiful, deep rust, lacy tattoo. We wanted to try it on ourselves. The henna women arrived at the house in giggles and we lay under the vine leaves on cushions, drinking mint tea while they painted. We had to remain there for several hours, immobilized, until the henna dried. Meanwhile the women, in a festive mood, prepared a *couscous,* which they brought to us on a low table. Because we could not use our hands (or even stand up), they had to feed us, rolling *couscous* deftly into balls and putting them into our mouths. We drank Oustalet, the splendid Moroccan rosé, and one of the women, although a Moslem and not supposed to drink, mixed hers with cola, half-and-half, and four teaspoons of sugar.

I have always loved Indian food. As children living abroad we used to have curry lunches—it was "not done" to eat curry in the evening. I can't remember why. Several different kinds of curry would be served buffet style on a large table with small bowls of condiments—chutneys, *raita* (yogurt dishes), chopped apples, bananas, raisins, coconut, peanuts, tomatoes, and onions—and various kinds of bread. It was an Anglicized version, of course, but it always looked and smelled good. At boarding school we would eat curry once every two weeks. Those we considered the weak and feeble would ignore our jeers and be served ground meat in gravy at the "mince" table. At the curry table we were served the hottest beef curries I have ever had. An Indian would probably have been horrified. The sauce was thickened with flour and certainly made from commercial curry powder, but I thought it was delicious. I always felt excitement on those days when, after morning classes, as we lined up in compulsory silence to file into the dining room, I would smell the rich aroma down the hall.

The traditional use of curry (which comes from the word *kari*, meaning sauce) grew out of a need to preserve meat in extreme heat. There are hundreds of different kinds from hot to mild, and traditional recipes vary greatly from region to region. The heart of all Indian cooking is the *masala*, the combination of spices that gives each dish its special flavor. *Masalas* may be "wet," spices ground with vinegar, water, or coconut milk (the base of dishes in the south) or "dry" (more commonly used in the north). Combining the spices correctly is a skill and the sign of a good cook. Basic spices include turmeric, a hard yellow root that is ground into a fine powder; cumin seed, whole or powdered; coriander seed; fenugreek; fennel seed; and saffron. Poppy and sesame seeds, nutmeg, cardamom, cloves, and cinnamon are common aromatics; chilies, onions, and garlic; and fresh herbs such as coriander, mint, and basil are also frequently used. Lemon juice, vinegar, and tamarind water, pomegranate seeds, and dried mango powder give added piquancy to Indian food.

Religion has had a major impact on Indian and Pakistani food. The predominantly Hindu population in India is vegetarian and their food is generally "hotter" than Moslem. Vegetables (known as *bhaji* in the north, *foogath* in the south) are commonly fried in spices with no sauce. Curries are made with one or more vegetables. Sometimes vegetables are shaped into patties and fried. Moslems in India and Pakistan eat plenty of meat—mainly beef, lamb, and chicken. They never eat pork. Specialties include *koftas* (spicy meatballs), *kormas* (braised meat cooked in yogurt or cream), *kebabs,* and *bhoonas* (meat sautéed, then baked). Pakistani specialties include *shami kebabs* (curried meatballs), chicken *tikka* (grilled chicken), *shish kebab,* and beef *biryani.*

In northern India, bread making is an art. Excellent breads accompany every meal and they are used to scoop up the thick, dry sauces. They are often spiced. Among the most impressive are *naan,* unleavened bread that is baked in a *tandoor,* a five-foot-deep clay jar oven; *chapattis,* unleavened griddle bread; *paratha,* a multi-layered spongy bread; *poori,* deep-fried puffs; and *pappadums* made from lentil flour.

One of India's finest dishes is chicken *tandoori.* The chicken is marinated for a day or two in yogurt and spices, then broiled in a *tandoor* oven, which gives it a crisp exterior while keeping it tender and moist inside.

Southern Indian sauces, more liquid than northern sauces, are generally eaten with rice. Particularly good are *vindaloo* dishes (lamb, chicken, or shrimp marinated in a combination of vinegar, spices, and chili peppers and simmered in the marinade). Coconut oil is the popular cooking fat. In the north *ghee,* or clarified butter, is used, and Bengalis prefer mustard oil.

Yogurt is eaten by Moslems and Hindus alike to aid digestion. It is often served plain or combined with diced vegetables and spices. *Dal* (lentils), of which there are nearly sixty varieties in India, are stewed and served as an antidote to hot curries.

Although the Indonesians share the Indians' penchant for curries, the distance covered by the 3,000 islands is responsible for inter-esting variations in Indonesian cuisine. Among the islands with a distinct culinary reputation are Java, Sumatra, Kalimantan (previ-ously Borneo), Sulawesi (Celebes), and Bali. Javanese food reflects its agricultural background. Sumatran dishes were created as a result of the heavy trade in spices and are liberally seasoned with dry seeds and aromatic spices. It was these spices—nutmeg, cloves, and mace as well as turmeric, pepper, ginger, and cinnamon—that were exported to Europe and the Middle East, where they altered the character of local cooking.

In Indonesian cooking today, the Arabs, Chinese, Spanish, and the Indians have all exerted their influences. Curries in Indonesia have fewer spices than their Indian counterparts. Coconut milk, chilies, onions, and turmeric are the basic ingredients. Flavoring agents include lemongrass, *laos, blachan,* or *trassi* paste (a shrimp paste), garlic, coriander, limes, citrus leaves, and cumin. A popular condiment to be found on almost every table is *ketjap,* an Indonesian soy sauce.

When the Dutch gained control of the Indonesian spice market, the *rijsttafel,* a feast of Indonesian dishes, became the symbol of Dutch colonialism. *Rijsttafel* is an awe-inspiring spread that may consist of twenty to thirty Indonesian specialties—fresh pineapple slices, fresh and fried bananas, dried shrimp, chopped peanuts, grilled meat, curries, *krupuk* (pounded shrimp fried in hot batter that puffs into curly flakes), mango chutneys, and various *sambals. Nasi goreng* (fried rice with chicken) is often served with heavily spiced fish, with accompaniments of cucumber relishes, gherkins, and fresh coconut. *Saté,* small chunks of meat or fish, are threaded onto wooden skewers, marinated and basted with soy sauce and oil, cooked over charcoal, and served with a pungent peanut sauce. To complement these divergent flavors, the Indonesians serve side dishes of raw or cooked salads and yellow rice cones decorated with chilies.

Another mélange of Chinese and Indian cuisines, with the emphasis more on the Chinese, exists in Malaysia and Singapore. Chilies in vinegar or fresh, chopped red chilies are frequently used as a garnish. Thai cooking is similar to Javanese—composed of many artfully decorated curries and Chinese dishes, with ingredients similar to those used by the Indonesians.

In the neighboring Philippine Islands, the cuisine has a distinct Spanish overtone. Food is less "hot"—paellas, sweet-sour stews, and grilled fish are typical.

The cooking of China ranks with the French as the finest in the world. There are five noted schools: Peking, Canton, Foochow,

Hunan, and Szechuan. Spices are used to enhance the flavor of food, not to mask it. Sesame oil; *hoisin,* plum, oyster, and soy sauces; dried mushrooms; bean paste; star anise; fermented black beans; Szechuan pepper; dried shrimp; and cloud ears (a dried fungus) are the most frequently used seasonings. Food is cooked in oil with garlic, scallions, and fresh ginger. The emphasis is on harmony and accent. Sweet is cooked with sour, crunchy with smooth; ingredients are seldom cooked alone, but combined to bring out the best in each other.

Cooking time is short for Chinese dishes; the preparation takes much longer. Ingredients are chopped in advance and cooked fast so that they retain their freshness. More pork is used than beef and the meat is generally cooked with vegetables. Few dairy products are eaten; vegetables and rice are the mainstays of a meal. Barley and wheat are also often used. Chinese vegetable cookery is the best in the world. It brings out the flavor and texture of the vegetables without destroying vitamins.

Although most Chinese dishes are cooked according to certain basic principles, China is such a vast country that there can be variations in local ingredients which give the impression of regional specialties. The inland province of Szechuan produces a pepper called *fagara*, a crop that is partly responsible for the hot, spicy food for which the region is famous. Food is cooked in oil with the pepper, which may not always seem fiery at first, but develops its heat almost as an aftertaste. Besides *fagara*, chilies are a major flavoring agent, as are garlic, scallions, five-spice powder (a ground blend of *fagara*, star anise, aniseed, cloves, and cinnamon), dried mushrooms and other fungi, ginger, and fennel.

Although there are no religious taboos preventing the Chinese from consuming lamb, it does not often figure in the diet. Pork, chicken, game, and fish from local rivers are the usual choices. Meat is often smoked or barbecued. Sometimes it is twice-cooked (first simmered and then stir- or deep-fried). The most renowned

Szechuan dishes are duck and pork; chicken with walnuts or hot peppers; spiced meat in a sauce delicately flavored with dried tangerine peel; hot and spicy carp; and pork with (imitation) fish flavor.

Hunan cooking is even "hotter" than Szechuan. The Yellow River running through this province is famous for its carp, which is served in a spicy sweet-sour sauce or in a hot bean sauce. Dry shredded venison in hot sauce is another popular Hunan dish.

Perhaps the widespread awareness of the insipidity of refined, mass-produced food has contributed to the trend in America toward highly seasoned cooking. When one is confronted with foods that have so little taste or flavor—vegetables grown for size, not quality; meat reared on hormones; standardized eggs—spices become almost indispensable. Even the most rural supermarkets have begun to stock spices and chilies on their shelves.

People who need to watch their intake of salt will find that spices will go far in making up for the lack of salt in their food. Add to this the fact that many spicy dishes are low in saturated fats and are actually quite light (and in this book I have used vegetable or olive oil wherever possible instead of lard or other saturated fats) and you have a type of cooking that is healthy as well as good to eat.

ORIGINS OF SPICES AND THEIR USE IN COOKING

〜〜 ALLSPICE 〜〜

This is not a mixture of spices, as some people believe. It is the berry of the allspice tree, which grows in the West Indies. Bought whole, and freshly ground with a pepper mill, it has a stronger flavor than in its packaged, powdered form.

It is a pungent and aromatic spice, tasting like a mixture of cinnamon, cloves, and nutmeg. It is used in curries and Mexican dishes and goes with most beef, lamb, and chicken stews.

〜〜 ANISE 〜〜

Anise is native to Middle Eastern countries. The seeds come from a plant with long, feathery leaves and taste of licorice. They are a natural stimulant and help counteract gas. Anise is said to aid the digestion and was used at the end of a meal by the Romans for such a purpose. Indians also employ the seeds as a pleasant-tasting *digestif*.

Anise is used in curries, stews, cheese dishes, and with fish.

〜〜 CARDAMOM 〜〜

Cardamom originated in India. It is the dried fruit of a plant belonging to the ginger family and one of the chief ingredients in curry powders. It has a strong, cool flavor and is mentioned in Sanskrit writings as preventing bad breath, headaches, fevers, coughs, colds, nausea, and even eye diseases. The greenish or straw-colored pods are usually discarded and only the tiny dark seeds inside are used in cooking. Cardamom is also very popular in Scandinavia. It was brought to Scandinavia from Constantinople by the Vikings and has been used there ever since.

Cardamom is used in preparing Indian food; it enhances fish, chicken, and fruit dishes. Arabs also use it to flavor coffee.

〰〰 CAYENNE 〰〰

Cayenne pepper consists of the ground seeds and pods of peppers that originally came from Cayenne in Africa. It helps the digestion. A small amount is excellent with egg and cheese dishes, sauces, and shellfish.

〰〰 CINNAMON 〰〰

The cinnamon tree is native to Ceylon and Malabar. The pungent fragrance of its bark comes from the oil, which has valuable uses in medicine. It is a stimulant, a carminative, and an astringent. It is also a preservative.

Cinnamon is used in many Southeast Asian, Indian, and Mexican dishes and in desserts and fruit sweets.

〰〰 CLOVES 〰〰

The clove tree is an aromatic evergreen that looks rather like a laurel. It grows principally in the Philippines, Molucca Islands, and Zanzibar. The dried, unopened flower buds were used to preserve foods in the Middle Ages and to mask the taste of rotting meat.

Cloves are a powerful antiseptic; they also sweeten the breath. Sanskrit writings describe the use of cloves against fever and stomach ailments, to stimulate the heart, and to help the functioning of liver and kidneys. They were also used as a local anesthetic, especially for a toothache. Cloves help digestion by accelerating the flow of gastric and intestinal juices.

They are used in Indian and Mexican cooking; in tomato, meat, and fish sauces; in soups and stews; and with fruit.

〰〰 CORIANDER 〰〰

Coriander spices many Mexican, Indian, and Indonesian dishes. It is native to southern Europe and the Near East. The plant has lacy leaves and looks like flat-leaved parsley.

The dried seeds have a fresh, delicate aroma that is best brought out when they are ground in a pepper mill immediately before use. Coriander is another basic ingredient in curry powder.

〰〰 CUMIN 〰〰

Cumin seeds are small and yellow-brown. They look and taste very much like caraway. Cumin is used for curry powders and chili powders and in Middle Eastern, Mexican, Indian, and North African cooking. Although available ground, the seeds are better bought whole and pulverized with a mortar and pestle. They are a valuable aid to the digestion.

Cumin is also good in bread; with cheese, eggs, meatballs, and hamburgers; and in pilaf and other rice dishes. It is an interesting complement to chicken, lamb, and eggplant.

〰〰 FENUGREEK 〰〰

Fenugreek is a tiny reddish brown seed that has a slightly bitter flavor and a sweet spicy scent when heated. It can be used powdered or ground.

Fenugreek too makes an important contribution to the characteristic flavor of curry powder and is a feature of many Indian dishes.

〰〰 GINGER 〰〰

Ginger is a root (or rhizome) used widely in Indian, Chinese, African, Caribbean, Mexican, and Southeast Asian dishes. It is one of the most ancient spices, said to have originated in south Asia and the East Indies. In its dried, powdered form, ginger is more pungent than when it is fresh. Jamaican ginger has a more delicate flavor and is by many considered the best.

An ancient remedy for warding off colds, ginger is a stimulant, carminative, and stomach remedy. Sanskrit writings mention it as a cure for anemia and liver complaints.

Fresh ginger is sliced or chopped into stews and Chinese dishes. It complements fish, meat, and poultry.

∿∿ HORSERADISH ∿∿

The piquant, biting taste of the horseradish root gives mustard its characteristic flavor. Freshness is essential in horseradish as it is apt to become bitter if kept more than a season. Its sharpness is a pleasant contrast to fatty meats.

∿∿ MACE AND NUTMEG ∿∿

Mace is the outer coating of the seed that grows on nutmeg trees in Sri Lanka, Sumatra, and Malaya. The Spice Islands, once under Dutch control, were the original source of nutmeg. The Dutch, to preserve their monopoly on this valuable spice, dipped the nutmegs in lime so that the English and French would not be able to plant the seeds.

Sold in powdered form, mace is mild and fragrant. It can often be substituted for nutmeg, although its flavor is somewhat stronger.

Nutmeg is best freshly grated—in the old days little nutmeg graters were worn around the neck by people who could afford the exotic spice. With cheese, vegetables, and curries it is subtle yet definite. Nutmeg is a reputed stimulant; known as a cure for colic, flatulence, and an aid to digestion.

∿∿ MUSTARD ∿∿

Mustard is an annual herb. It grows in Europe, Asia, and North Africa and wild in much of the United States. The seed can be dark red or yellow. Whole mustard seed is not as hot as ground mustard.

Commercial dry mustard is often a blend of both; sometimes turmeric is added to heighten the yellow. Prepared mustard is a paste made with vinegar or wine, sugar, and herbs. In some intangible way, mustard ingredients reflect national temperaments. French mustard is usually mixed with white wine or vinegar; German with tarragon vinegar and spices; English mustard, like Chinese mustard, is a paste made from plain mustard powder mixed with water.

In sauces, with meats, fish, vegetables, and pickles, mustard is popular seasoning.

∿∿ PAPRIKA ∿∿

Paprika comes from a species of capsicum plant that is cultivated in Central America, parts of Europe, and the United States. The pepper was taken to Europe by Columbus, who discovered it in the Caribbean Islands.

Hungarian paprika is the most renowned; it is the strongest and consists of the whole pod, seeds, and stems of the dried red pepper. A mild Spanish paprika is the one most commonly used in the United States. Its *raison d'être* is color and garnishing.

Paprika is the only known dry source of vitamin C, and a tablespoon is said to equal the juice of four lemons. Recent research has found paprika to be high in carotene and vitamins A, B, B_2 and P, which is important in the prevention of arteriosclerosis. Paprika stimulates the appetite, increases the flow of gastric juices, and has been used in treatment of bronchitis, pleurisy, and joint and nerve afflictions.

∿∿ PEPPER ∿∿

Black pepper, often confused with peppers of the Capsicum family, is a berry that grows principally in India, Southeast Asia, and the East Indies. In the Middle Ages it was a source of wealth and was used to pay taxes. Henry II imposed levies of pepper, which in those days approached the value of gold or silver. The Portuguese monopoly on the pepper trade lasted well into the eighteenth century.

Pepper comes in several forms: powdered, coarsely ground, and whole peppercorns. White pepper is merely pepper with the outer coating of the seed removed. The innovation of white pepper was aesthetically inspired: to some people black grounds in a white sauce are as distressing as black tar on a white beach.

〰〰 SAFFRON 〰〰

Saffron is the dried stigma of an autumn crocus, native in Asia and parts of Europe. It is the most expensive spice in the world. More than 200,000 stigmata are needed to make a pound. It has a warm, bitter aroma and a golden color and is sold powdered in small envelopes or in tiny orange and gold threads. Some of these powders are adulterated with turmeric. Saffron rice is a popular dish in Indian and Asian cooking. The spice is also used in stews and curries.

One of the earliest known spices, saffron was very popular in Europe and used by the Babylonians, the Greeks, and the Indians. In medieval England it was used as a hair dye. Buddhist monks use it to dye their robes.

In ancient and medieval times, saffron was thought to revive the spirit and to prevent fainting fits and palpitations of the heart.

〰〰 TURMERIC 〰〰

Turmeric is native to India and other parts of Asia. It is a dried aromatic root or rhizome related to the ginger family. The brilliant yellow of turmeric varies in hue from canary to saffron. Moroccan dishes get their characteristic color from turmeric, which is an ingredient of curry powder (also used in sauces and rice).

SOME ORIENTAL
ᗯᗯ FLAVORING AGENTS ᗯᗯ

FISH SAUCE: A bottled sauce available in Chinese markets, containing fish extract, water, and salt. It is useful for flavoring soups, stews, and sauces.

KETJAP MANIS: This is an Indonesian soy sauce, sweeter than the Chinese variety.

LAOS: Available whole or in powdered form in Indonesian specialty stores; *laos* is the root of a Malayan plant related to ginger.

SEREH OR LEMONGRASS: An aromatic, lemon-scented tropical grass, available dried as a powder or in blade form, and fresh in Hawaii and Puerto Rico.

TRASSI: A thick Indonesian shrimp paste, *trassi* has a strong smell and keeps almost indefinitely. It should be stored in a closed container.

CHILI PEPPERS

Within a century after their discovery in the New World, peppers and chilies altered the character of national cuisines. Used as vegetables or spices, peppers and chilies are of the Capsicum family. Hundreds of varieties range from mild and sweet (the bell pepper) to fiery (Hungarian paprika capsicum). Red peppers are green peppers that have matured on the vine. Red chilies, most frequently sold dried, produce quite a different effect from the green ones, which are available fresh or canned.

Both red and green chilies are used in the native cuisines of Mexico, Indonesia, Malaysia, Thailand, India, Pakistan, parts of Africa, and China. They have a high vitamin content and are often munched whole. The Peruvian Indians of the Andes have a chili so hot that the smallest quantity will transform an otherwise bland dish.

Chilies are essential to certain relishes, chutneys, *sambals,* and Latin American hot sauces. Few of the recipes in this book insist on a particular variety except in cases where a recipe simply would not be right with a substitute—Mexican *mole poblano,* for example. In these instances powdered, canned, fresh, or dried chilies are specified. The following is a list of chilies generally available in the United States; most of the names are in Spanish.

∿∿∿ DRIED RED CHILIES ∿∿∿

CHILE ANCHO: A large chili, with a color ranging from dark red to almost black and a taste ranging from quite mild to *picante*. It is often confusingly labeled *pasilla.* This chili is ground and used in chili powders. It is also soaked and used as a paste, a sauce, or relish.

CASCABEL: So called because it sounds like a rattle when you shake it. This small round chili has a brownish red skin like a *guajillo* chili (the two are often confused) and a pleasant nutty flavor.

CAYENNE: A long thin pepper, very hot, used to make cayenne pepper.

CHIPOTLE: A dried, smoked *jalapeño* chili that is light brown or brick red in color. It is used in *salsa* and egg dishes, to season soups or stews, and is often sold canned, preserved in vinegar.

GUAJILLO: A long, narrow, light red-hot chili that is often sold pickled. It is also sometimes called *cascabel.*

HONTAKA: A Japanese chili, longish, medium size and red-hot.

MULATO: A brownish black chili, similar in shape to the *ancho,* with a sweeter flavor. It is used in *mole* and other Mexican sauces. It is often confused with the *ancho* chili.

PASILLA: Also known as *chile negro* in California. It is a long slender chili, much darker than *ancho* chilies, with less flavor but more bite. It is used toasted and ground for table or cooked sauces.

PEQUÍN: A very small and very potent red-hot chili, used dried as a relish or in *salsas.*

ᴧᴧᴧ GREEN CHILIES ᴧᴧᴧ

CALIFORNIA GREEN CHILI: Also known as Anaheim, it is bright green, about 6 inches long and 1½ inches wide. It has a firm, thick flesh and mild taste.

NEW MEXICO GREEN CHILI: Also known as Anaheim, *chile verde,* and Big Jim. Similar in shape to the California Anaheim; medium-hot to hot in flavor.

GÜERO: A small yellow chili, very hot, used as a salad and in sauces.

JALAPEÑO: A small round chili about 2½ inches long and ¾ inch wide. It is sold green and red and ranges from hot to very hot. It is also sold canned. Substitute fresh *chile serrano* if *jalapeño* is not available.

POBLANO: A large dark green, shiny chili not widely available in the eastern United States, sometimes called *mulato* or even *pasilla*. It has a mild full flavor (and can be quite hot). California Anaheim, green bell, or Italian peppers can be substituted but the taste will not be the same. When ripened and dried, this chili becomes known as *chile ancho*.

SERRANO: A small light green chili, sometimes very thin, less than ½ inch wide. The skin has a strong flavor and the seeds are very hot. *Jalapeño* chilies can be substituted.

PREPARING CHILIES

To prepare fresh chilies, run them under cold water and cut off the tops, remove the seeds and the veins if they are large. They can be peeled and scraped after charring over a gas flame, and then wrapped in a towel. This makes them soft for cooking in sauces and enhances their flavor.

Dried chilies should be torn into small pieces and soaked in boiling water for half an hour before being used. About a cup of water to six chilies is the usual proportion (this applies only to recipes using dried chilies that are not ground to a powder). The chilies are then put in a blender with their soaking liquid and puréed.

Chili powder is a blend of ground seeds and pods from dried chilies mixed with other herbs and spices such as cumin, garlic, oregano, and cayenne pepper. See page 30 for Homemade Chili Powder. The powder you buy varies a lot in potency. Do not keep powders for over a year—they lose their vitality. A spice grinder comes in handy for dried chilies; it quickly reduces them to a fine powder. A tablespoon of powdered chili equals one whole chili. Cayenne can be used in place of *chile pequín*. *Ancho, mulato,* and *pasilla* chilies are available in powdered form in specialty shops.

Pepper flakes are made by grinding dried red chilies very coarsely, usually with the seeds.

To reduce the strength of a chili, remove the seeds. Fresh chilies can be made milder by being soaked in salted water for a while before being used.

Canned chilies should be rinsed in cold water to remove the brine.

You can sting yourself if you touch chilies with your bare hands and then touch your mouth, eyes, or nose. For this reason, it is advisable to wash thoroughly with soap and water after handling chilies.

THE
HOT & SPICY
KITCHEN

ᴡᴡᴡ EQUIPMENT ᴡᴡᴡ

It *is* possible to live without a corn popper or a waffle iron. There are, however, certain items that should be included in every kitchen. The following is a basic list.

POTS AND PANS

Use a heavy, cast-iron frying pan or the French kind with a copper bottom. Cast-iron pans need not be washed if the food has not been cooked in animal fat (this includes, of course, butter). They can be wiped out with paper towels and salt. Iron pans should be left overnight with a layer of oil in them before they are first used; otherwise they may get rusty.

Casseroles made from enameled cast iron are the best, although the very large ones can be extremely heavy. Cast-iron casseroles are particularly versatile because they can be used both on top of the stove and in the oven.

Unglazed pottery casseroles with tightly fitting lids, available in French specialty stores, Mexican shops, and in Morocco (where they are known as *tajins*), are excellent for stewing. They, too, should be soaked with oil before they are used.

A wok is not an essential piece of equipment but it is extremely useful, particularly for stir-frying food. It is a round, concave pan, and it should be washed and carefully dried after being used. Do not fill it more than a third full when you are using it or the food will spill out when you stir.

A steamer is excellent for cooking vegetables. A simple fan-shaped insert usable with most saucepans can be bought for very little in dime stores. This can also be placed in a deep frying pan.

A collapsible salad basket will serve this function too. A spaghetti cooker or a *couscoussière* will also perform the double duty of steaming vegetables.

KNIVES

A cleaver is good for chopping vegetables. French cleavers are smaller than Chinese cleavers and not quite as menacing. Knives should be kept very sharp. The flint method is the most effective. Carbon-steel knives keep their points better than stainless steel but they have a tendency to rust.

OTHER EQUIPMENT

A slotted spoon is good for removing food from sauces or water.

A set of measuring spoons and cups. Aluminum is more efficient than plastic.

A bulb baster. Again, aluminum is better than plastic, which tends to melt at the tip.

Iron trivets are prettier and safer than asbestos mats under pans to prevent food from burning. Incidentally, avoid thin aluminum pans and glassware because they burn food unless carefully watched.

A set of wooden spoons.

A wire whisk.

Mixing bowls in assorted sizes.

A butcher's block or thick chopping board, which should be placed near the stove.

Plenty of washable pot holders.

A roasting pan with a rack.

A blender or food mill for making purées. A mortar and pestle or small spice grinder for spices.

An oven thermometer.

A meat thermometer.

ᨊᨊ **KITCHEN HINTS** ᨊᨊ

HOW TO PREPARE TOMATOES AND GREEN PEPPERS

Roll the whole tomatoes or peppers over a gas flame until the skin is charred all around. Tomatoes can be peeled immediately. Peppers should be wrapped in a dishcloth and left for few minutes. Unwrap, peel off the skin, cut in half, and remove the seeds. Then chop or leave halved, according to recipe.

Tomatoes can also be peeled after being dropped into boiling water for a couple of minutes. I prefer the charring method because it gives the tomato a charcoal flavor.

USING HERBS

Put fresh herbs into a cup and chop them with a pair of kitchen scissors.

Powdered herbs have less flavor than crumbled leaves. Store away from light.

Fresh basil, tarragon, rosemary, and thyme can be grown in small pots on a kitchen windowsill. Chives are the only herbs that take well to freezing. Basil can be frozen and used in stews but it loses much of its flavor and the color goes off.

CHOPPING GARLIC

Smash the garlic, with the skin on, with the flat side of a knife. Then peel and chop.

If you choose to use a garlic press, leave the skin on the garlic. When you come to clean it, lift out the skin (the garlic will have been pressed through, leaving the skin inside) and you will find that the bits of garlic that generally get stuck in the holes of the press will come out with it in one piece.

USING FRESH GINGER AND HORSERADISH

Both of these can be frozen. Peel them and wrap them in foil. Grate while frozen hard.

SALT

Sea salt or rock salt ground in a small wooden grinder is the best. Kosher salt is good too.

SEEDS AND NUTS

Sesame seeds are delicious baked dry in the oven and sprinkled on food.

Ground pumpkin seeds, almonds, hazelnuts, walnuts, pine nuts, and sesame seeds are excellent as sauce thickeners.

BREAD CRUMBS

These can be in the blender with toasted or fresh bread and stored in the refrigerator in a jar. Toast can also be turned into bread crumbs if you put it in a paper bag and hammer it with a rolling pin.

OIL

The best sesame oil is Chinese. Health food stores sell a variety without much flavor. This, along with light oils such as safflower or peanut, is the best for frying foods when you do not want a dominant oil flavor.

POWDERS, PASTES
& BASICS

I once came across a letter in the food section of a newspaper in which a woman complained that the food editor always asked for freshly ground pepper in her recipes. "I am a busy housewife," she wrote, "and I do not have time to grind pepper every time I cook." One wondered why she bothered to cook at all and what kinds of meals she must have served. She was missing one of the most enjoyable aspects of cooking. There is great satisfaction in grinding spices or pounding them with a mortar and pestle, smelling the rich aroma that rises as their oil is released.

Spices can be ground in a blender or small spice grinder. Like coffee, they lose their oil and flavor if left for a long time after they have been ground. A small pepper mill will grind coriander seeds, mustard seeds, and allspice successfully, although it will not reduce them to the fine powder some recipes demand. Whenever possible, one should buy spices whole and grind them at home.

Curry paste should not be used as a substitute for curry powder; use only where specified in the recipes. Curry powder is not a spice, as some people still believe, but a blend of spices. The powder usually contains, among other ingredients, turmeric, coriander, mustard seed, allspice, and chili. Indian families grind and mix their own, making it as mild or hot as they please. Commercial curry powder varies, but by and large it has a harsh medicinal taste and is made with inferior spices.

This chapter also includes simple chili pastes and powders, recipes for spiced oils and vinegars, and mixed ground spices, some of which can be made and stored until needed. It also includes a section on staples for certain spicy recipes such as coconut milk, homemade yogurt, *ghee,* tamarind water, and so on, which are referred to throughout this book.

∿∿∿ MADRAS CURRY POWDER ∿∿∿

This is a hot, pungent curry powder.

4 dried red chilies (pages 13–14)
4 tablespoons coriander seed
5 tablespoons cumin seed
2 tablespoons peppercorns
3 tablespoons turmeric
½ teaspoon mustard seed
½ teaspoon fenugreek
2-inch cinnamon stick
6 cardamom seeds
2 tablespoons cloves

Combine the ingredients in a blender or spice grinder and grind until fine.

∿∿∿ MILD CURRY POWDER ∿∿∿

1 tablespoon turmeric
2 tablespoons ground mace
2 tablespoons ground cloves
4 tablespoons peppercorns
2 tablespoons peeled cardamom seeds
4 tablespoons cumin seed
2 bay leaves
1 dried red chili (pages 13–14)

Roast all the ingredients for half an hour in a 200-degree oven. Grind in a spice grinder or blender.

ᗯᗯ GARAM MASALA ᗯᗯ

This is an aromatic powder that can be used as a basis for curries or for marinating meat. It can also be sprinkled on food just before you serve it.

½ cup cardamom seeds
2 tablespoons ground cinnamon
¼ cup ground cloves
4 tablespoons ground mace
4 tablespoons coriander seed
¼ cup peppercorns
3 tablespoons black cumin

Roast the cardamom seeds in a 200-degree oven for half an hour without browning. Remove the pods and combine in a blender or spice grinder with the remaining ingredients. Grind very fine.

ᗯᗯ SIMPLE GARAM MASALA ᗯᗯ

¼ cup cloves
¼ cup peppercorns
3 tablespoons peeled cardamom seeds
1 tablespoon ground cinnamon

Combine ingredients in a blender or grinder and mix well.

ᗯᗯ MASALA WITH CHILIES ᗯᗯ

2 dried red chilies (pages 13–14)
½ cup coriander seed
1 tablespoon cumin seed
2 tablespoons turmeric

In a blender or grinder combine chilies, coriander seed, cumin, and tumeric. Turn the mixture out onto a piece of foil and bake in a 250-degree oven for about half an hour.

∿∿∿ INDIAN VINDALOO PASTE ∿∿∿

This paste makes a hot sweet-sour curry.

1 medium onion, coarsely chopped

2 cloves garlic, coarsely chopped

1 tablespoon turmeric

2 tablespoons coriander seed

1 teaspoon ground red chilies

½ teaspoon mustard seed

¼ teaspoon fenugreek

1 teaspoon ground ginger

1 teaspoon cumin seed

Vinegar to make a paste

Put the onion and the garlic in the jar of an electric blender or chop finely and put in a mortar to grind with pestle. Grind the spices in a spice grinder and combine with the onion mixture. Add enough vinegar to make a paste and blend, adding more vinegar, if needed, to make a thick, stiff paste. Use as directed in recipes.

∿∿∿ INDIAN CURRY PASTE ∿∿∿

This will keep better if you use *ghee* (see page 38) instead of butter. It is a fairly hot paste.

4 dried red chilies (pages 13–14)

4 tablespoons coriander seed

1 tablespoon cumin seed

2 tablespoons black pepper

2 tablespoons coarse salt

1 tablespoon mustard seed

Grind all the dry ingredients. Combine in a blender with remaining ingredients and mix to a smooth paste.

½ tablespoon saffron
   threads soaked in 3
   tablespoons hot water
1 clove garlic, crushed
½ cup vinegar
¼ cup *ghee* (page 38) or
   butter

〰〰 THAI CURRY PASTE 〰〰

A medium-hot paste. It can be made in a blender or with a mortar and pestle, the dry ingredients being ground first and made into a paste with the juice from the shallots and chilies.

**4 dried red chilies,
   ground, or 4 green
   chilies, chopped (pages
   13–16)
2 shallots, chopped
1 clove garlic, chopped
1 tablespoon *trassi* (page
   9)
1 teaspoon *laos* powder
   (page 9)
1 tablespoon *sereh*
   powder (page 9)
1 tablespoon paprika
1 teaspoon cumin seed
1 teaspoon coriander seed
Grated rind of 1 lemon
Coarse salt**

Combine all the ingredients in a blender and purée. If using green chilies, omit the paprika.

∿∿∿ INDONESIAN VINDALOO PASTE ∿∿∿

Use this paste for hot curries.

6 green chilies (pages 14–15)
½-inch piece of fresh ginger, chopped
2 cloves garlic, chopped
1½ teaspoons ground coriander seed
1 teaspoon ground cumin
¼ teaspoon turmeric

Grind all ingredients in a blender, adding a little water to the mixture to obtain a smooth paste.

∿∿∿ HOMEMADE CHILI POWDER ∿∿∿

3 *pequín* chilies (page 14)
3 *ancho* chilies (page 13)
1½ tablespoons cumin seed
1 teaspoon oregano

Combine all ingredients in a blender or grinder.

∿∿∿ RED CHILI PASTE ∿∿∿

This paste can be used in recipes as a substitute for fresh chilies. It will keep for 2 to 3 weeks refrigerated.

8 dried red chilies
Boiling water to cover
¼ cup olive oil
1 clove garlic, peeled
Coarse salt
1 cup boiling stock

Open chilies and remove seeds. Cover with boiling water and leave to soak for 2 hours. Drain. Combine in blender with oil, garlic, salt, and stock. Reduce to smooth purée.

〜〜 MILD YELLOW CHILI PASTE 〜〜

This paste can be used in recipes calling for a mild chili flavor. It will keep refrigerated for 2 to 3 weeks.

2 dozen yellow fresh
  ***güero* chilies,**
  blanched, rinsed under
  cold water, and seeded
  (page 14–15)
2 tablespoons peanut or
  vegetable oil
2 tablespoons vinegar
Coarse salt

Combine all ingredients in a blender and reduce to a smooth purée.

〜〜 SPICED PEPPER 〜〜

Use with steaks, roasts, or grilled chicken.

4 tablespoons coarsely
  ground pepper
2 tablespoons thyme
1 teaspoon garlic powder
1 tablespoon Hungarian
  paprika
1 teaspoon caraway seeds

Combine all ingredients.

∿∿ RAS EL HANOUT ∿∿

This is a mixture of spices used in Moroccan dishes, particularly in *tajines* (Moroccan stews). In Moroccan markets, variations of this mixture are sold already ground. Because many of the authentic ingredients are not available in the United States, I am providing a simplified version that you can make yourself. Keep it in a tightly sealed jar. It is also delicious as a flavoring for non-Moroccan meat and vegetable dishes.

½ **tablespoon ground mace**

½ **tablespoon allspice**

10 cardamom seeds, peeled

1 whole nutmeg (or 1 tablespoon, ground)

½ **tablespoon** *laos* **root (page 9)**

½ **tablespoon black peppercorns**

½ **tablespoon white peppercorns**

1 tablespoon ground ginger

½ **tablespoon ground cinnamon**

2 whole cloves

1 teaspoon turmeric

1 teaspoon aniseed

Use a spice grinder to combine the spices.

〜〜 **ORIENTAL CHILI OIL** 〜〜

This is a hot sesame-scented oil. Use it sparingly as a dipping sauce for spring rolls and dumplings and to sprinkle on top of stir-fried foods. It will keep in the refrigerator indefinitely.

⅓ cup Oriental sesame oil
⅔ cup peanut oil
1 tablespoon dried red
   chili flakes

Combine the oils in a small, heavy saucepan. Heat for a few minutes then add a few chili flakes to test. If they foam—without turning black— add the tablespoon of chili flakes and remove the pot from the stove. Cover and let cool. If the flakes turn black, however, remove the pot from the heat and cool until flakes tested will foam but not blacken.

Strain the oil through cheesecloth and store in a glass jar. Refrigerate unless you have a cool dark place to store the oil. Bring it to room temperature before using.

 **YIELD: 1 CUP**

〰️ ACHIOTE OIL 〰️

This is not hot, but it gives food the red-orange color and subtle flavor characteristic of Caribbean and Latin American dishes. *Achiote* seeds (also called *annatto* seeds) are available in Latin American specialty stores and some supermarkets. This oil can be used for frying meat or fish.

1 cup of peanut or vegetable oil

¼ cup of *achiote* seeds

Heat oil in a saucepan, then add *achiote* seeds. Cover, turn down heat, and cook for a minute. Cool, strain, and keep the oil in a tightly sealed jar in the refrigerator.

〰️ SPICED VINEGAR 〰️

Use in salads and any other dish calling for vinegar that might benefit from this spicy flavor.

1 pint white wine vinegar
1 teaspoon cloves
1 teaspoon peppercorns
2 teaspoons sugar
1-inch piece of fresh ginger, sliced
2 dried red chilies (pages 13–14)

In a saucepan combine white wine vinegar (retain the bottle for later use) with cloves, peppercorns, ginger, and 1 teaspoon of the sugar. Add remaining sugar to taste and chilies. Bring to a boil. Cover and simmer for 2 minutes, remove from heat, and return to the bottle.

∿∿ PIRI-PIRI ∿∿

AFRICAN CHILI OIL

Use for frying foods that would benefit from a subtle chili flavor or for basting grilled meats and poultry.

1 cup olive, vegetable, or peanut oil

4 or 5 fresh or dried red chilies (pages 13–16)

Heat oil and pour into a jar that contains the chilies. Seal tightly and keep for a month before using.

∿∿ KENYA HOT PEPPER SHERRY ∿∿

Similar to a condiment used in the Caribbean, this keeps indefinitely and is used for flavoring soups and stews.

4 or 5 fresh hot chilies (pages 13–16)

Dry sherry

Put chilies in a quart glass jar and fill it up with sherry. Let stand, tightly sealed and away from the light, for a month before using.

∿∿ TAMARIND WATER ∿∿

Tamarind is sold as a paste in Indian and Indonesian stores and is often used in preparing dishes native to these countries. The paste keeps indefinitely and is well worth buying.

1 cup water

1 tablespoon tamarind paste

Bring the water to boil and pour it over the paste and mix well.

ᴡᴡᴡ COCONUT MILK ᴡᴡᴡ

Coconut milk is not difficult to make and it is worth the time. It is used as a "stock" for many Indian, Caribbean, and Southeast Asian dishes and can be frozen. It keeps for up to a week in the refrigerator. To buy coconuts, choose the heaviest ones and shake to see how much liquid there is inside. Don't buy coconuts with soft or wet "eyes." A 1½-pound coconut should yield about 3 to 4 cups of milk.

1½-pound coconut
Hot water

To open a coconut, puncture the eyes and pour the coconut water into a bowl. Heat oven to 400 degrees and bake the coconut for 15 minutes. Remove it, put it on a hard surface, and split with a hammer. The meat should come off easily (the heating is not necessary but it makes it easier).

You can now grate the coconut meat (peeling off the skin) or put it through a mincing machine. It can also be ground with water in a blender and the water then drained off.

Measure the amount of coconut water and put equal amounts of hot water with the coconut into a blender. Blend until you have a thick liquid.

Strain the liquid through a cheesecloth. The simplest way is to put it in a sieve and leave it over a bowl for a few hours. Press it down with a wooden spoon to squeeze out the remaining liquid and discard the pulp.

For a richer milk, refrigerate for an hour or so, until it separates. Once separated use only the top, skimming it off like cream. The remaining milk can be used in stews. Desiccated coconut can be used with milk or water, but the resultant milk will be thinner. Soak coconut for an hour in hot water or milk using about ½ cup meat to 1 cup liquid.

ᐟᐟᐟ HOMEMADE YOGURT ᐟᐟᐟ

Yogurt is one of the simplest things to make. Having for years messed with yogurt makers and expensive cultures, I eventually discovered what seems to be the cheapest and easiest way to produce good homemade yogurt. You simply take a spoonful of plain commercial yogurt and add it to approximately a pint of warmed milk. If the milk is too hot it will kill the culture. Put your finger in the milk; if you can keep it there and slowly count to ten without it burning, the milk is cool enough. Pour it into a thermos flask. Leave it for about 8 hours and your yogurt should be done. It may need longer to set at the beginning. Each time you want to make more yogurt, add a little of the last batch to warmed milk.

I bring the milk to a boil to kill any bacteria that may interfere with the yogurt bacteria, and let it cool, covered so that a skin does not form.

For a thick yogurt, powdered milk may be added.

You can use yogurt in curries, stews, sauces, or salad dressings, or serve it on its own as a cool accompaniment to spicy food.

Yogurt can also be made by keeping the mixture warm on the back of the stove or in a warm oven (not hot or the bacteria will be destroyed). Yogurt makers are really glorified hot plates. They keep the yogurt warm and at a constant temperature.

∿∿ GHEE ∿∿

Ghee is clarified butter and used in Indian cooking. When the butter is heated and kept simmering, the milk solids separate from the fat. The solids are strained off carefully, leaving the clear fat, which keeps for up to three months at room temperature. It is particularly useful for frying because it burns at a far higher temperature than butter and gives an interesting nutty flavor to the food.

1 pound butter

Melt butter without browning it over a medium flame and bring it gently to the boil. Skim off the white foam that rises to the surface, reduce heat, and simmer gently, uncovered, for 45 minutes until the milk solids on the bottom are brown and the butter on top is clear and transparent.

Strain the butter through a sieve lined with 4 layers of cheesecloth. If it is not perfectly clear, strain again. Store in an airtight jar.

SOUPS

This chapter contains recipes for hot and cold soups, some of which are substantial enough to constitute a main course. Do not overspice soup or use commercial curry powder. The individual spices should permeate the mixture. When the soup is made the day before, its flavor improves and becomes more pronounced.

Keep grated coconut and chopped almonds or peanuts on hand to garnish these soups. Dried vegetables should be washed and picked over before being cooked. Although it is not necessary to soak them in advance, doing so cuts down cooking time. Because foam that accumulates tends to make the soup bitter, you should be careful to skim off any that rises to the surface.

Don't take shortcuts when you are preparing soup. You will only be disappointed with the results. It is very important to have a good stock. Bouillon cubes will not do the trick. Stocks can be made from leftover meat, chicken, fish, and vegetables and then frozen until you need them. The following stocks are also good for gravies and stews.

〰 CHICKEN STOCK 〰

The finished stock can be frozen for up to six months. It is more useful to freeze it in several small containers rather than in a single large one.

1 2- to 3-pound chicken
1 large onion, cut in quarters
1 leek, sliced (optional)
4 carrots, cut in chunks
3 stalks celery with leaves, cut in chunks
Herb bouquet (thyme, bay leaf, and parsley tied in cheesecloth)
1 tablespoon black peppercorns
1 teaspoon coarse salt

Place the chicken in a large stockpot with the remaining ingredients and cover with enough cold water to come an inch above the meat. Bring to simmer, skimming off any scum that accumulates.

Turn down heat and simmer gently for 3 hours. Strain, discarding the solids, cool, and refrigerate. When the stock has chilled, remove the fat, which will have risen to the top in a lump.

 **YIELD: ABOUT 2 TO 3 QUARTS**

〰 FISH STOCK 〰

Ask for fish heads, bones, and tails from your fishmonger. You will probably get them free. Do not use dark-fleshed fish such as mackerel, sardines, bluefish, or whitefish. White-fleshed fish such as bass, snapper, sole, flounder, halibut, cod, or tilefish is the best. For a shellfish stock, add lobster and/or shrimp shells.

4 pounds fish heads and bones
1 large onion, sliced

Use a large heavy casserole—not an aluminum pot—and put in all the ingredients and enough water to

Herb bouquet (thyme, bay
leaf, and parsley tied in
cheesecloth)
1 teaspoon black or white
peppercorns
1 cup dry white wine
1 teaspoon coarse salt

come an inch above the fish heads. Simmer gently, partially covered, for 40 minutes. Do not cook longer or the stock may turn bitter.

Strain, discarding any solids, and cool. Chill until ready for use or turn into small containers and freeze.

❧ **YIELD: ABOUT 2 QUARTS**

〰 COLD CURRIED SOUP 〰

4 tablespoons butter
1 large onion, diced
2 celery stalks with leaves,
chopped
1 tablespoon Mild Curry
Powder (page 26)
1 tablespoon flour
2 apples, peeled and
chopped
About 1 cup cooked
chicken meat, chopped
5 cups Chicken Stock
(page 42)
Juice of half a lemon
Coarse salt and freshly
ground white pepper
1 cup heavy cream
Fresh chopped chives to
garnish

Melt the butter in a saucepan and gently cook the onion and celery without browning until soft. Add the curry powder and flour and cook for a couple of minutes, stirring.

Either combine the onion-curry mixture in a blender with the apples, chicken meat, and a cup of chicken broth or put it through a food mill with the apples and chicken. Return the purée to the saucepan and add the remaining broth, lemon juice, salt, and pepper. Bring to a boil, remove from heat, and chill overnight.

To serve, pour the chilled soup into individual bowls, spoon the cream on top, and garnish with the chives.

 SERVES 6

∿∿ CURRIED LENTIL SOUP ∿∿

This is a filling soup and needs only a salad such as Turkish Cucumbers in Yogurt (see page 230) and cheese to follow. Indian bread or dark bread and unsalted butter are good with it. Homemade *Chapattis* (see page 217) can be prepared while the soup is cooking.

2 tablespoons butter or ghee (page 38)
2 onions, chopped
2 potatoes, diced
1 to 1½ tablespoons Mild Curry Powder (page 26)
½ pound dried lentils
4 cups vegetable or chicken stock
Juice of half a lemon
Coarse salt and freshly ground pepper
Heavy cream (optional)
Fresh chopped parsley or mint to garnish

Heat the butter in a heavy casserole and sauté the onions and potatoes until golden. Add the curry powder and cook for a few minutes. Add the remaining ingredients (except parsley and cream) and simmer for an hour, skimming off any foam that may rise to the top. Put the mixture through a food mill (or purée in a blender) if you would like a smooth soup. Return to the casserole, bring to a boil, and serve. A little cream may be poured into each bowl of soup and the parsley or mint sprinkled on top.

 SERVES 4

〰〰 CHILLED CURRIED PEA SOUP 〰〰

When fresh peas are in season this is an excellent way to use the large peas that appear on the market. Serve with grilled fish or chicken, lamb chops, kidneys, or liver as a main course.

2 tablespoons butter
1 clove garlic, chopped
1 medium onion, chopped
1 tablespoon Mild Curry
Powder (page 26)
¾ pound shelled peas
1 leaf of lettuce, quartered
2 cups Chicken Stock
(page 42)
1 cup heavy cream
Juice of half a lemon
Coarse salt and freshly
ground pepper
Fresh chopped chives,
mint, basil, to garnish

Melt the butter in a saucepan and soften the onion and the garlic without browning. Add the curry powder and cook for 2 minutes. Add the peas, lettuce, and 1 cup of the chicken stock. Bring to a boil, reduce heat, and simmer for 15 minutes. Purée in a blender or sieve the mixture.

Return the mixture to the saucepan and add the remaining stock. Simmer for 5 minutes. Remove from the heat and add the cream, lemon juice, and salt and pepper to taste. Chill.

To serve, pour the chilled soup into individual bowls and garnish with a tablespoon of extra cream, if you like, and the chopped herbs.

 **SERVES 4 TO 6**

⩘⩘ BLACK BEAN SOUP ⩘⩘

1 pound black beans
Water to cover, plus about
  4 cups
1 onion, coarsely chopped
1 carrot, sliced
3 celery stalks with leaves,
  coarsely chopped
Herb bouquet (parsley,
  thyme, and bay leaf tied
  in cheesecloth)
4 whole allspice
2 whole cloves
¼ teaspoon ground mace
¼ teaspoon ground
  cinnamon
2 cloves garlic, chopped
1 fresh green chili,
  chopped (pages 14–15)
Coarse salt and freshly
  ground pepper
¼ cup rum
Lemon slices
Sour cream

Soak the beans overnight. Simmer in water with vegetables, herbs, and spices for about 3 hours, adding water if necessary. Stir in the rum, bring to a boil, and pour into heated soup bowls. In each bowl, put a spoonful of sour cream and a slice of lemon.

 SERVES 8

⋀⋀⋀ JAMAICAN RED PEA SOUP ⋀⋀⋀

Red kidney beans can be used here. The ones used in Jamaica are smaller and similar to Mexican chili beans.

1 pound dried red beans
Water to cover
2 onions, chopped
¼ pound salt pork
4 tablespoons chopped
 parsley
½ teaspoon thyme
2 celery stalks with leaves
2 fresh chilies, chopped
 (pages 13–16)
Coarse salt and freshly
 ground pepper

Simmer the beans for 2½ to 3 hours with the remaining ingredients. Add more water, to cover, as they cook. Purée in a blender or put through the coarse blade of a food mill. Return to pan and correct seasoning.

❧ SERVES 6

⋀⋀⋀ HUNGARIAN ONION SOUP ⋀⋀⋀

A good stock is essential for this soup. Serve it with black bread.

4 large onions
3 tablespoons butter
2 teaspoons Hungarian
 paprika
6 cups chicken or beef
 stock, homemade
2 tomatoes, peeled and
 chopped (page 21)
½ teaspoon oregano
Coarse salt and freshly
 ground black pepper

Slice the onions and soften them in the butter in a large, heavy saucepan. Sprinkle with paprika and cook for 2 minutes. Add the remaining ingredients and simmer gently for an hour. Correct seasoning and serve.

❧ SERVES 6

〰 CHICKEN SOUP WITH RICE 〰

The soup itself is not hot but the *sambal* that goes with it as a relish is. This is more of a stew than a soup and certainly constitutes a main course. A salad to follow would be plenty. It is also an attractive dish for entertaining; the garnishes can be arranged on a plate or in little bowls and add color to the table.

SOUP

1 3- to 4-pound chicken
Water to cover
Coarse salt and freshly
  ground black pepper
1 medium onion, chopped
½-inch piece of fresh
  ginger, chopped
2 tablespoons macadamia
  nuts, chopped
1 tablespoon peanut or
  vegetable oil
1 teaspoon turmeric

GARNISHES

Rice (pages 211–212)
Chopped or sliced
  hard-boiled eggs
Shredded cabbage
Potato chips, crushed
Chopped celery
Slices of lemon

SAMBAL

2 chopped *serrano* chilies
  (page 15)

To make the soup, simmer the chicken in water to cover with salt and pepper until it is done. Remove, cool slightly, and bone. Meanwhile fry the onion, ginger, and macadamia nuts in the oil and add with the turmeric to the simmering broth.

Return the boned chicken to the soup, bring to a boil, remove from heat, and serve with the garnishes and *sambal,* to which people help themselves at the table.

The *sambal* is made by combining the chilies, ginger, and vinegar and adding enough chicken broth to make it fairly liquid.

 **SERVES 4 TO 6**

2 tablespoons chopped
   fresh ginger
1 tablespoon vinegar
Chicken broth to moisten
   as needed

〰〰 SPICY TOMATO SOUP 〰〰

1 medium onion, chopped
2 tablespoons butter
1 clove garlic, minced
2 green bell peppers,
   chopped
1 tablespoon flour
1½ pounds tomatoes,
   peeled and chopped
   (page 21)
4 cups chicken or
   vegetable stock
½ teaspoon crushed
   coriander seed
½ teaspoon Tabasco
   sauce
¼ teaspoon
   Worcestershire sauce
3 teaspoons freshly
   grated horseradish
Dash tarragon vinegar to
   taste
Coarse salt and freshly
   ground pepper
Fresh chopped parsley or
   basil to garnish
Croutons to garnish

Soften the onion in the butter with the garlic and peppers in a large, heavy-bottomed saucepan. Add the flour and cook for 2 minutes without burning. Add the remaining ingredients (except garnishes) and simmer gently for about 1½ hours. Correct seasoning, sprinkle on parsley or basil and croutons, and serve hot.

🍃 SERVES 4

∿∿ HOT AND SOUR SOUP ∿∿

After this Chinese soup you may want to continue with a Chinese meal. Twice-Cooked Szechuan Pork (see page 166) or Chicken in Chili-Walnut Sauce (see page 136) served with rice and Chinese-style vegetables would follow very well.

If you have leftovers, such as thinly sliced cooked pork, beef, duck, chicken, or shrimp add them at the end so that they heat through without becoming overcooked.

4 dried black Chinese mushrooms
¼ pound lean pork
2 ½-pound bean curd cakes
4 cups beef or chicken stock
2 tablespoons dry sherry
2 tablespoons vinegar
1 teaspoon soy sauce
½ teaspoon Tabasco sauce
Coarse salt and freshly ground pepper
2 tablespoons cornstarch mixed to a paste with 2 tablespoons cold water
1 egg, beaten
About 1 tablespoon sesame oil
1 scallion, chopped

Soak the mushrooms in water for half an hour. Drain, reserving the liquid, and slice into thin strips. Slice the pork and the bean curd in strips. Bring the stock to the boil and simmer the pork and mushrooms for 10 minutes. Add the bean curd and simmer for a couple more minutes. Add the sherry, vinegar, soy sauce, Tabasco sauce, salt, pepper, and cornstarch mixture. Simmer for a few minutes until thick. Remove from heat and add the egg, stirring constantly. Add the oil and scallion, mix in, and serve.

🌶 **SERVES 4**

⋙ SHRIMP AND VEGETABLE SOUP ⋙

Follow this Southeast Asian soup with grilled meat or chicken served with rice. Be careful not to overcook the shrimp, 3 or 4 minutes is plenty, and remember that it will go on cooking even after the soup has left the stove.

1 medium onion, chopped
1 clove garlic, chopped
2 *serrano* chilies, minced
  (page 15)
2 tablespoons peanut,
  vegetable, or coconut oil
1 teaspoon coriander
  seed, ground
4 cups Coconut Milk
  (pages 36–37)
1 pound diced vegetables
  (sweet corn, French
  beans, peanuts, zucchini,
  eggplant, etc.)
½ pound peeled shrimp
1 teaspoon grated lemon
  rind
Coarse salt and freshly
  ground pepper

Fry the onion, garlic, and chilies in the oil until golden. Add the coriander and fry for 2 minutes, stirring. Add the coconut milk and the vegetables and simmer, covered, until vegetables are just tender. Add the shrimp, lemon rind, salt, and pepper and cook for a few minutes—just enough barely to cook the shrimp. Serve hot.

🌺 SERVES 4

ᐯᐯᐯ SPICY GAZPACHO ᐯᐯᐯ

Use the best ripe tomatoes available for this refreshing summer soup. The soup is chilled overnight and the garnishes are handed around in small bowls, to be sprinkled on top of the soup.

1½ pounds fresh ripe tomatoes
1 small onion, cut in pieces
2 to 3 fresh *jalapeño* chilies (pages 14–16)
1 green bell pepper, seeded and quartered
2 Kirby cucumbers or 1 small cucumber, peeled and cut in pieces
4 sprigs fresh coriander (or more to taste)
3 tablespoons red wine vinegar (or more to taste)
1 clove garlic, chopped
1 teaspoon sugar
2 cups tomato juice
Diced cucumber, onion, green pepper, avocado, and tomato to garnish
Chopped coriander leaves to garnish
***Tostado* chips**

In several steps if necessary, place the ingredients for the soup in a food processor and process until minced and combined. Taste and adjust seasonings.

Chill overnight and serve, passing the garnishes and the *tostado* chips separately.

 SERVES 6

HORS D'OEUVRES

Some of the hors d'oeuvres in this chapter are suitable for handing around with drinks before dinner; others are good as first-course dishes or lunch entrées. Hot, spicy hors d'oeuvres are particularly good in the summer with tall drinks. Many of the dishes in this chapter—*tacos, anticuchos,* spareribs, and *satés,* for example—are delicious cooked outside over charcoal and served with dips and sauces on the side.

Marinated raw fish dishes from Latin America and the Caribbean are excellent light starters to an evening meal and can be made in advance.

ᗯᗯ **TACOS** ᗯᗯ

Tacos are tortillas, usually fried, wrapped around chopped meat, sometimes folded and secured with a toothpick, sometimes simply folded over. They lend themselves to a variety of fillings: chopped meat, mashed beans, diced chicken or fish, cheese, chopped lettuce, chopped tomato, etc. For a party you can arrange bowls of Mexican sauces on the table, Mexican Refried Beans (see page 207), *Guacamole* (see page 67), chopped meat, fresh and canned chilies, chopped onion, and a plate of hot tortillas—all to be eaten with the fingers.

Tacos are also good in a complete Mexican meal, which might include a meat or chicken dish, *Enchiladas* (see pages 203–205), Mexican Beans (see page 206), Fried Ripe Plantains (see page 191), Mexican Refried Beans (see page 207), and rice.

FILLINGS

CHEESE TACOS: Fill with slices of Monterey Jack (or similar cheese), diced *jalapeño* chilies (see pages 14–15), chopped tomatoes, salt, and pepper.

HAM TACOS: Fill with diced ham that you have mixed with diced onion, cream cheese, and chopped *jalapeño* or *serrano* chilies (see pages 14–15).

SWEET PEPPER TACOS: Soften chopped bell peppers and onions in oil, add some peeled tomatoes, a little sour cream, salt, and pepper, and heat through.

CHORIZO TACOS: Fill with chopped, skinned, fried *chorizos* that you have mixed with an equal amount of diced cheese (Monterey Jack or similar).

BEAN TACOS: Fill with leftover Mexican Refried Beans (see page 207) and cheese, with diced *jalapeño* chili (see pages 14–15).

PICADILLO TACOS: Fill with leftover *Picadillo* (see page 151) or make the recipe using half the quantity.

Stuff the tortillas. Heat about a tablespoon peanut or vegetable oil in a large, heavy skillet. Fry the *tacos*, turning once, until golden. Drain on paper towels and serve hot.

NOTE: If tortillas are dry, soften them before stuffing by dipping them in warm oil.

∿∿ CALIFORNIA TACOS ∿∿

A light snack, an hors d'oeuvre, or a party dish, *tacos* are simple to make and can be prepared (except for the final frying) in advance. Use quantities according to how many people you are feeding.

Tortillas

Chopped lettuce

Chopped chilies

Chopped onions

Chopped tomatoes

Grated cheddar cheese

**Coarse salt and freshly
ground pepper**

Fry the tortillas in a light oil, fill them with the vegetables and cheese, season with salt and pepper, and fold one side of the tortilla over to form a kind of sandwich. Serve hot.

∿∿ CHILI CASHEWS ∿∿

**1 pound shelled, plain
cashews**
2 tablespoons peanut oil
1 teaspoon chili powder
**¼ teaspoon dried ground
chilies (pages 13–16)**
Coarse salt

Fry the nuts in the peanut oil until golden brown. Sprinkle with the chili powder and ground chilies while hot. Season with coarse salt.

∿∿ CHEESE STRAWS ∿∿

GREAT BRITAIN

1½ cups white flour
Coarse salt
**¼ teaspoon Hungarian
paprika**
**½ teaspoon cayenne
pepper**
12 tablespoons butter
**1½ cups grated Parmesan
and cheddar cheese
(mixed)**
**¼ teaspoon Tabasco
sauce**
1 egg yolk

Sift the flour and add the salt, paprika, and cayenne. Rub in the butter until the mixture is like oatmeal. Add the cheeses, Tabasco sauce, and egg yolk. Make into a smooth dough, adding water as necessary. Roll out onto a floured board and cut in narrow strips, about ¼ inch wide and 3 inches long. Bake in preheated oven at 400 degrees for about 7 to 8 minutes, or until golden.

 YIELD: ABOUT 20 CHEESE STRAWS

∿∿ DEVILED ALMONDS ∿∿

1 pound shelled, skinned almonds
Salt to taste
Cayenne pepper to taste

Preheat oven to 300 degrees. Roast the almonds on a baking sheet, turning from time to time, until they are golden. Remove from the oven, sprinkle with salt and cayenne pepper, and cool.

∿∿ JAMAICAN PLANTAIN CHIPS ∿∿

Serve these with drinks or with spicy grilled meat. Use plantains that are green or half ripe.

Plantains
Oil for deep frying
Coarse salt

Slice the peeled plantains into rounds. Heat the oil until it registers 375 degrees on a frying thermometer. Fry the plantains until crisp. Drain on paper towels. Sprinkle with salt before serving.

❧ **YIELD: ABOUT 10 CHIPS PER PLANTAIN**

ᜠᜠ MOROCCAN CARROTS ᜠᜠ

Flat Arabian bread (pita) goes with this hors d'oeuvre. *Tahini* (sesame paste) and Greek feta cheese are also available at Arab specialty shops and make a good opening spread. Afterward, perhaps roast or grilled lamb, or kabobs and a green vegetable.

1 pound carrots, peeled and cut in quarters
Water to cover
4 tablespoons olive oil
1 tablespoon vinegar or lemon juice
Coarse salt and freshly ground pepper
½ teaspoon cumin seed
1 teaspoon cayenne
2 tablespoons fresh chopped parsley to garnish

Simmer the carrots in water until barely tender. Remove and coat with the olive oil mixed with the vinegar. Season with salt, pepper, cumin, and cayenne. Sprinkle with parsley and serve when cool.

ᜠᜠ MOROCCAN-STYLE OLIVES ᜠᜠ

Use cracked green olives. These are unripe olives, cracked and soaked in brine. Those available in the United States should be washed, drained, and boiled before being marinated.

½ pound green olives
Juice of 2 lemons
2 cloves garlic, minced
1 tablespoon paprika
¼ teaspoon dried ground chilies (pages 13–16)

Put the olives in an earthenware dish, combine the remaining ingredients and pour onto the olives. Let stand overnight at room temperature before serving.

½ teaspoon cumin seed
2 tablespoons olive oil
½ cup chopped fresh
  parsley
Coarse salt to taste

ᨆ⋀ ALBÓNDIGUITAS ⋀ᨆ

LITTLE MEXICAN MEATBALLS

Serve these with toothpicks and a Mexican sauce.

1 tablespoon peanut oil or
  butter
1 medium onion, finely
  chopped
2 slices white
  homemade-type bread
½ to ¾ cup milk
1 pound ground beef
½ pound ground pork
2 eggs
1 tablespoon chili powder
Coarse salt and freshly
  ground pepper
2 tablespoons minced
  fresh parsley or
  coriander
Oil for frying

Heat the oil and cook the onion until soft but not browned. Meanwhile soak the bread in the milk.

In a large bowl combine the onion, bread (squeeze milk out before using), meat, eggs, chili powder, salt, pepper, and parsley. Form into bite-size balls.

Heat the oil in a skillet and fry the balls until browned and cooked through. Drain and serve hot.

❧ YIELD: 30 MEATBALLS

NOTE: Another way to cook these is in a stock made from meat and tomato juice. Simmer them with enough liquid to cover for about 45 minutes. Drain and reserve the stock for other uses.

〰〰 MARINATED SPICY BEEF STRIPS 〰〰

Marinate the beef overnight. Serve the strips with toothpicks, with the sauce in a separate bowl as a dip.

MARINADE

1 clove garlic, chopped
1 medium onion, chopped
2 tablespoons finely
  chopped fresh ginger
1 teaspoon crushed red
  chili peppers
2 teaspoons soy sauce
½ cup peanut or
  vegetable oil
Dash Tabasco sauce

MEAT

1 pound lean steak (any
  cut)

SAUCE

2 tablespoons sugar
½ cup red wine vinegar
3 tablespoons plum jam
2 tablespoons mango
  chutney
Dash Worcestershire sauce
Coarse salt and freshly
  ground pepper

To make marinade, combine the ingredients in a bowl large enough to hold the meat.

To prepare the meat, cut it against the grain into the thin strips about 2½ inches long and ½ inch wide. Put the meat in the bowl with the marinade and marinate overnight.

Make the sauce the night before by combining all the sauce ingredients and refrigerate.

Heat the oil in a skillet, remove meat from marinade, and place in the skillet. Stir-fry over high heat for about 2 minutes. Do not overcook or the meat will curl and toughen. Pour any juices from the skillet into the sauce, mix, and serve.

 **SERVES 4 TO 6**

〰️ **MUSHROOMS PAPRIKASH** 〰️

This Hungarian hors d'oeuvre is delicious on toast or served in little pastry shells that have been filled and heated through in the oven.

3 tablespoons unsalted butter

2 tablespoons chopped shallots

1 pound mushrooms, sliced

Coarse salt and freshly ground pepper to taste

2 teaspoons Hungarian paprika

1 teaspoon flour

½ cup sour cream

Fresh chopped parsley to garnish

Melt the butter in a large frying pan and soften the shallots without burning. Add the mushrooms and salt and cook for about 5 minutes, or until the juices begin to form. Add the pepper, paprika, and flour and cook for another 2 minutes, stirring. Add the sour cream and cook just long enough to heat through, remove, and serve with chopped parsley on top.

 SERVES 4

〰〰 **PANUCHOS** 〰〰

These miniature tortilla snacks originate in Yucatán. They are simple to make and are good as an appetizer or light lunch dish.

12 4-inch tortillas
½ recipe for Mexican Beans (page 206) or Mexican Refried Beans (page 207)
3 hard-boiled eggs, sliced
2 whole cooked chicken breasts, boned and diced
Grated fresh Parmesan or cheddar cheese
Red Pepper Sauce (page 250)

Make a slit in each tortilla and fill the pocket with the beans and a slice of egg. Fry in the lard or oil. Drain on paper towels. Serve topped with chicken and cheese, the sauce spooned on top.

🌶 **YIELD: 6 SERVINGS**

〰〰 **WELSH RAREBIT** 〰〰

Cheddar cheese and cayenne pepper are very good together. Rarebit is best made with a good dry, aged cheddar, brown ale, and spiced with cayenne and hot mustard.

½ pound aged cheddar
1 tablespoon butter
½ cup brown ale
Coarse salt and freshly ground pepper
½ teaspoon Dijon mustard
Cayenne pepper to taste

Slice or coarsely grate the cheese. Heat it over low heat and add the remaining ingredients, stirring constantly until you have a smooth paste. Serve at once.

 🌶 **SERVES 4**

CHILIES STUFFED
～～～ WITH CREAM CHEESE ～～～

Stuffed and sliced thinly, these fiery little peppers are delicious on rounds of dark bread or crackers.

Small canned or fresh red or green chili peppers (pages 13–16)
Cream cheese
Coarse salt to taste
Chopped walnuts

Cut off the caps and remove the veins and the seeds from the chilies.

Mash the cheese with the salt and walnuts and stuff the mixture into the chilies. Refrigerate for a few hours.

Slice the chilies very thinly with a sharp knife and place on buttered bread or crackers.

～～～ DEVILED SARDINE CANAPÉS ～～～

2 cans of skinless and boneless sardines, packed in oil
Juice of 1 lemon
Dash Tabasco sauce
1 teaspoon Dijon mustard
½ teaspoon cayenne pepper
Coarse salt and freshly ground pepper
6 slices homemade-type bread (white or whole-wheat)

Mash sardines with lemon juice, Tabasco sauce, mustard, cayenne pepper, salt, and pepper. Spread mixture on buttered toast fingers and place under a broiler until sizzling. Serve hot.

❧ YIELD: 12 TOAST FINGERS

⋁⋀⋁ LIPTAUER KÄSE ⋁⋀⋁

This can be served in a mound, sprinkled with paprika, so that guests help themselves and spread the mixture on black or rye bread, or it can be used as a spread for canapés.

1 cup cottage cheese

1 stick butter, at room temperature

2 anchovies, drained and finely chopped

1 tablespoon capers, chopped

1 tablespoon caraway seeds

1 tablespoon chives, chopped

1 tablespoon dry mustard

1 tablespoon Hungarian paprika

½ teaspoon celery salt

Mash all the ingredients together and shape into a mound. Sprinkle with extra paprika. This will keep for several days in the refrigerator.

 **YIELD: 1¼ CUPS**

∿∿ GUACAMOLE ∿∿

Use the dark-skinned pebbly Haas avocados; they have more taste than the smooth-skinned variety.

4 ripe avocados

4 tablespoons finely chopped scallion or red onion

2 medium tomatoes, seeded and chopped

2 to 3 *serrano* or *jalapeño* chilies (according to taste), charred, peeled, seeded, and finely chopped (pages 14–15)

½ teaspoon chili powder

½ cup fresh coriander leaves, chopped

¼ cup extra virgin olive oil

Coarse salt and freshly ground pepper to taste

Lemon or lime juice to taste

Halve and pit the avocados and cut the flesh in small pieces. Place in a bowl and add the remaining ingredients (except the lemon juice). Mix together lightly so the *guacamole* is slightly chunky.

Squeeze the lemon juice over the top to prevent the mixture from turning brown. Decorate with a sprig of coriander and serve at room temperature.

✌ **YIELD: ABOUT 2 CUPS**

ᐸᐸᐸᐸ PERUVIAN SEVICHE ᐸᐸᐸᐸ

For this popular Peruvian hors d'oeuvre, raw fish is marinated in lime and lemon juice, which turns it white and "cooks" it. Serve the fish on oiled lettuce leaves.

2 pounds raw fish (sole, red snapper, or any white-fleshed fish)
3 to 4 hot red or green chilies (pages 13–16)
1 cup lime juice
1 cup lemon juice
Coarse salt and freshly ground pepper
Fresh chopped coriander leaves
Lettuce leaves
1 medium onion, cut in rings

Bone the fish and cut it into 2-inch pieces. Chop the chilies finely and put in a bowl with the lime and lemon juice. Add the fish, season, and mix thoroughly. Leave for several hours, or overnight if possible. To serve, sprinkle with coriander and serve on lettuce garnished with onion rings.

❦ **SERVES 6 TO 8 AS AN APPETIZER**

ᐸᐸᐸᐸ SCALLOP SEVICHE ᐸᐸᐸᐸ

1 pound raw bay scallops
1 cup fresh lime juice
1 small onion, chopped
2 *serrano* or *jalapeño* chilies, chopped (pages 14–16)
2 tablespoons chopped fresh parsley
½ cup extra virgin olive oil

Cut the scallops into quarters and cover with the lime juice. Marinate overnight. Add the remaining ingredients and season to taste with salt and freshly ground pepper. Serve with toothpicks as an hors d'oeuvre, or as an appetizer with dark bread or tortillas.

❦ **SERVES 4**

∿∿ SEVICHE SALAD ∿∿

An expanded version of *seviche*, this contains tomatoes and peppers. Serve it on oiled lettuce leaves with slices of avocado sprinkled with lemon juice and Spanish onion rings if you like.

2 pounds raw fish (see above)

1 medium onion, chopped

3 to 4 hot red or green chilies, chopped (pages 13–16)

1 clove garlic, chopped

1 cup lime juice

1 cup lemon juice

Coarse salt and freshly ground black pepper

1 red bell pepper

1 green bell pepper

1 tomato, peeled, seeded, and chopped (page 21)

Bone the fish and cut it into 2-inch pieces. Combine it in a bowl with the onion, chilies, garlic, lime juice, and lemon juice. Season and leave to marinate for a few hours or overnight.

Slice the bell peppers and add to the fish with the tomato. Toss and arrange on lettuce.

❧ **SERVES 8 AS AN APPETIZER**

NOTE: You can vary this salad by adding chopped capers, chopped parsley, coriander leaves, or a dash of Tabasco sauce.

HUBERT'S SOFT-SHELL CRABS
〰〰 **NAMBAN** 〰〰

Len Allison, the chef at Hubert's in Manhattan, serves this as a first course, marinating cooked crabs in a sauce made with sake, *ponzu* (a Japanese citrus sauce available in Oriental markets), chilies, onion, and garlic.

CRABS

12 soft-shell crabs, cleaned

Flour for dredging

About ¼ cup sesame oil

About ¼ cup vegetable oil

1 large red onion, thinly sliced

2 to 3 tablespoons flying fish roe to garnish (optional)

MARINADE

1 cup sake

2 cups *ponzu*

1½ cups light soy sauce

½ ounce fresh ginger cut in julienne

1 *jalapeño* chili, left whole (pages 14–15)

1 clove garlic, peeled and left whole

Clean and dry the crabs. Heat the oils in a large skillet or wok to 180 degrees. Dredge the crabs with the minimum amount flour and sauté in the oil for 2 to 3 minutes on each side.

To make the marinade, combine sake, *ponzu*, soy sauce, ginger, chili, and garlic.

Put the crabs and red onion in the marinade and let sit for 1 to 2 hours. To serve, quarter the crabs and, if you like, place the flying fish roe on top to garnish.

 SERVES 4

〰 SHRIMP REMOULADE 〰

Serve this on or with thin slices of toast.

**1 pound shrimp, cooked
and peeled**
**1 cup Homemade
Mayonnaise (page 249)**
3 teaspoons Dijon mustard
**1 tablespoon chopped
capers**
**1 tablespoon chopped
gherkins**
**1 tablespoon chopped
fresh tarragon**
**1 tablespoon chopped
fresh parsley**
**½ teaspoon anchovy
paste**
**Coarse salt and freshly
ground pepper**

Marinate the shrimp for 1 or 2 hours
in a mixture of the remaining ingredients.

 **SERVES 4 AS AN APPETIZER**

ᗯᗯ **DEVILED SOFT ROES** ᗯᗯ

A British dish, this is good either as an hors d'oeuvre or as a light lunch. In Britain it is often served at the end of a meal as a savory.

½ pound soft roes
Flour for dredging
Coarse salt and freshly
  ground pepper
Cayenne pepper
Dry mustard
2 tablespoons butter
Lemon juice
Toast

Dredge the roes in flour that you have highly seasoned with salt, pepper, cayenne, and mustard. Heat the butter and fry the roes on either side. Squeeze on plenty of lemon juice and serve on buttered toast.

❧ **SERVES 4 AS AN HORS D'OEUVRE**

ᗯᗯ **DEVILED CRAB AU GRATIN** ᗯᗯ

You can also serve this as a main dish, followed by a salad.

4 cooked crabs
1 tablespoon butter,
  melted
2 tablespoons fresh, white
  bread crumbs
1 tablespoon freshly
  grated Parmesan cheese
½ cup heavy cream
Worcestershire sauce
Dash Tabasco sauce
½ teaspoon Dijon mustard
Dash cayenne
Coarse salt and freshly
  ground pepper

Put the crabmeat in a bowl with the remaining ingredients. Mix thoroughly, put the mixture into the crab shells, dot with extra butter, and dust with extra Parmesan and cayenne. Bake in a preheated 375-degree oven for about 15 minutes.

❧ **SERVES 4**

ᐺᐺᐺ SCANDINAVIAN MUSTARD HERRING ᐺᐺᐺ

You may use salted herring that has been soaked or herring marinated in vinegar and sold in jars. This dish is great for lunch with hard-boiled egg slices and new potatoes, or served on black or rye bread like a Danish open sandwich. To serve it as an hors d'oeuvre, I suggest you accompany it with slices of fresh black bread and unsalted butter.

4 herring, sliced

2 tablespoons Dijon mustard

½ cup olive oil

½ cup heavy cream

1 tablespoon brown sugar

1 tablespoon vinegar

3 tablespoons diced pickle or capers

Coarse salt and freshly ground white pepper

1 tablespoon fresh chopped chives

Arrange the herring on a serving platter. Combine the mustard, oil, cream, sugar, vinegar, pickles, salt, and pepper. Pour over the herring and sprinkle with chives.

 SERVES 4

∿∿ **ANTICUCHOS** ∿∿

These little beef heart kabobs are sold like hot dogs in the streets of Peru. They are marinated in a mixture of spices and grilled over charcoal after being threaded on tiny cane skewers. You may also use liver, kidneys, beef, chicken, or seafood.

MARINADE

1 cup red wine vinegar
2 cloves garlic, chopped
1 tablespoon cumin
Coarse salt and freshly
ground pepper

ANTICUCHOS

1 beef heart
2 fresh red chilies, diced
(pages 13–16)
1 tablespoon *achiote*
seeds
½ cup olive oil

To make marinade, combine the ingredients.

To make the *anticuchos*, trim the filaments from the beef heart and cut it into 1-inch cubes. Marinate the beef overnight.

Soak the chilies, torn into small pieces, in boiling water to cover for half an hour. Put the *achiote* seeds in a blender and grind to a powder (or use a pestle and mortar). Add the chilies with their liquid and the oil. Blend.

Cook the beef pieces, threaded on skewers, over charcoal or under a broiler. Combine three-quarters of the marinade with the *achiote* mixture and baste the beef hearts with this as they are cooking. Serve immediately.

NOTE: *Achiote* seeds are red, irregularly shaped little seeds that can be bought in Latin American specialty stores and some supermarkets.

⋁⋁⋎ INDONESIAN SATÉ ⋁⋁⋎

Saté is a little kabob. It can be served either as an hors d'oeuvre or as a main course. Beef, lamb, pork, kidneys, liver, fish, or chicken are cut in ¾-inch cubes, marinated, and threaded on small wooden skewers. They are then broiled over charcoal and served with a variety of sauces, most of them piquant. The skewers should be soaked in water before they are used or they will burn.

Satés can also be served accompanied by rice, various *sambals* (see pages 264, 265, and 266), chutneys (see pages 261–263), and slices of orange.

⋁⋁⋎ CURRIED STUFFED EGGS ⋁⋁⋎

6 hard-boiled eggs
3 tablespoons Homemade
 Mayonnaise (page 249),
 or commercial
 mayonnaise can be used
3 or 4 scallions, chopped
½ cup chopped, cooked
 shrimp
Coarse salt to taste
1 tablespoon Mild Curry
 Powder (page 26)
Paprika to garnish

Cut the eggs in half and remove the yolks. Mash the yolks in a bowl with the remaining ingredients except the paprika, adding more mayonnaise as needed to obtain the right consistency. Fill the whites with the mixture, sprinkle with paprika, and arrange on a serving plate.

⌇⌇⌇ CRABES FARCIS ⌇⌇⌇

GUADELOUPE

This works very well with fresh lump crabmeat. Arrange the mixture in crab shells in the manner of *Coquilles Saint-Jacques*.

6 crabs

1 chili pepper, minced (pages 13–16)

3 tablespoons chopped fresh parsley

3 tablespoons chopped fresh chives

2 cloves garlic, minced

1 tablespoon lime juice

1½ cups fresh bread crumbs

Coarse salt and freshly ground pepper

¼ teaspoon ground allspice

3 tablespoons dark rum

Cayenne pepper

Butter

Cook the crabs in boiling water for 8 to 10 minutes. Cool. Remove the meat from the shells and claws and chop. Scrub the shells and set aside.

Combine the chili pepper, herbs, garlic, lime juice, 1 cup of the bread crumbs, and crabmeat in a mixing bowl. Season and add the allspice and rum. Mix thoroughly. Sprinkle with remaining bread crumbs and cayenne pepper, dot with butter, and bake in a 375-degree oven until lightly browned.

 **SERVES 6 AS AN HORS D'OEUVRE**

ᴠᴠᴠ MEXICAN SPARERIBS ᴠᴠᴠ

Pork ribs found in Mexico have much less fat than those found in the United States. The juices will most likely be too greasy to scrape up into a sauce. See the chapter on sauces for a dipping sauce. The ribs can be served on a plate with the dipping sauce in the middle and eaten with your fingers.

2 pounds pork ribs
Juice of 1 lemon
Coarse salt and freshly
**   ground pepper**
2 cloves garlic, sliced
1 medium onion, chopped
3 tomatoes, chopped
1 teaspoon sugar
2 teaspoons chili powder
Water as needed

Trim excess fat off the ribs and squeeze the lemon juice over them. Season them and place them in a roasting pan with the garlic and onion. Add the tomatoes and sprinkle the ribs with sugar and chili powder. Pour in enough water to cover the bottom of the pan and bake the ribs at 350 degrees in a preheated oven for about 1½ hours, or until crisp. Baste frequently with the sauce, adding more water if it dries up.

 **SERVES 4 TO 6 AS AN HORS D'OEUVRE**

EGGS

The best breakfast I ever had was in Yucatán. Before the day heated up we headed for a café that overlooked the harbor. As we watched the boats come in, we would eat fried eggs served on black beans and fresh tortillas, surrounded by peas sprinkled with cheese and accompanied by a hot tomato-chili sauce. The eggs were not the anemic productions unworthy of their name, with shells like paper, that have taken over the American market today. They were free-range eggs with bright orange yolks.

Because there is no pleasure in a plain boiled "chicken-factory" egg, spices have come to play a very important role in the art of egg cookery. This chapter features dishes that are acceptable for breakfast, lunch, or dinner. Don't, however, substitute commercial curry powder or skimp on ingredients.

ᗡᗡᗡ YUCATÁN EGGS ᗡᗡᗡ

6 tablespoons peanut oil

8 tortillas

½ recipe Mexican Beans (page 206)

8 eggs

½ recipe Salsa De Jitomate (page 246)

2 cups cooked green peas

4 tablespoons grated Parmesan or cheddar cheese

Coarse salt and freshly ground pepper

Bottled hot chili sauce to taste

Heat the oil in a large skillet and fry the tortillas. Spread them with a layer of hot beans and keep warm. Fry the eggs and place an egg on top of each tortilla. Spoon the tomato sauce over the eggs and arrange the peas around them. Sprinkle with cheese, correct seasoning, and sprinkle on chili sauce.

SERVES 4 (2 EACH)

⌇⌇⌇ MEXICAN SCRAMBLED EGGS ⌇⌇⌇

Cook the eggs extremely slowly over very low heat, stirring constantly.

8 eggs

2 tablespoons heavy cream

Coarse salt and freshly ground pepper

2 tablespoons butter

1 small onion, chopped

½ red or green bell pepper, chopped

1 tomato, peeled and chopped (page 21)

1 tablespoon chili powder

1 tablespoon fresh chopped coriander

Beat the eggs with the cream and season them with salt and pepper. Melt the butter in a heavy-bottomed pan and gently soften the onion with the pepper. Add tomato and the chili powder, cook for 2 minutes, then add the eggs, turning the heat down as low as it will go. Do not overcook the eggs; they should be slightly runny when you take them off the flame. Sprinkle with coriander.

 SERVES 4

∿∿ FLAMENCA EGGS ∿∿

This Spanish dish can be made in individual ramekins or in a large casserole. Using 1 egg per person, it makes a pretty hors d'oeuvre served in the individual casseroles. For a main course, a large dish with 2 eggs per person is simpler.

Chorizos can be bought in Spanish or Mexican specialty stores or homemade. Italian hot-pepper sausage is a good substitute.

4 *chorizos*

2 green bell peppers, chopped (page 21)

1 tablespoon butter

2 tablespoons olive oil

5 tomatoes, peeled and chopped (page 21)

Coarse salt and freshly ground pepper

8 slices smoked ham

1 pound peas, cooked

Slice the sausages thinly and fry with the peppers in butter and olive oil. Add the tomatoes and cook for 3 minutes. Season and set aside.

In a buttered dish arrange a layer of ham, peas, and tomato mixture. Make a little indentation for each egg and break in the eggs. Finish with a little more tomato sauce and bake in a moderate oven until the eggs are set.

✻ SERVES 4 AS A MAIN COURSE

NOTE: Use 4 eggs as an hors d'oeuvre and 8 as a main course.

〰〰 **HUEVOS RANCHEROS** 〰〰

A superb dish for a late Sunday morning breakfast. The eggs can either be cooked in the chili mixture or fried separately.

5 tablespoons peanut oil

1 medium onion, chopped

1 clove garlic, chopped

4 tomatoes, peeled and chopped (page 21)

2 chopped fresh chilies (pages 13–16) or chili powder to taste

Coarse salt and freshly ground pepper

4 tortillas

4 eggs

4 tablespoons grated Parmesan or cheddar cheese

1 avocado (optional)

Heat 2 tablespoons of the peanut oil in a skillet. Add the onion and garlic and cook until soft. Add the tomatoes and chilies and simmer until thick. Season.

In a separate pan heat the rest of the peanut oil and fry the tortillas. Remove and drain. Fry the eggs (or make hollows in the sauce and break them in, cover and cook over low heat until done). Put an egg on each tortilla, spoon on some sauce, sprinkle with cheese, and garnish with slices of avocado.

 **SERVES 2 TO 4**

〰️ HUEVOS CON CHORIZO 〰️

Chorizos (hot sausages) are available at Mexican or Spanish groceries. Italian hot sausage can be substituted.

1 tablespoon oil or butter

2 *chorizos*, skinned and chopped

1 medium onion, finely chopped

3 tomatoes, peeled and chopped (page 21)

Coarse salt and freshly ground pepper

1 fresh green chili, minced (pages 14–16) (optional)

6 eggs, lightly beaten

Heat the oil in a heavy-bottomed skillet. Fry the sausage meat with the onion for about 5 minutes. Add the tomatoes, salt, pepper, and chili and cook for another 5 minutes. Stir the eggs into the mixture and cook over low heat, stirring with a wooden spoon for about 3 minutes.

 SERVES 3

〰️ SPANISH PEPPER OMELET 〰️

Omelets are an ideal late breakfast or lunch dish. Serve with a tomato and onion salad made with Spanish oil.

1 red bell pepper

1 green bell pepper

1 fresh or canned green chili pepper (pages 14–16)

6 eggs

Coarse salt and freshly ground pepper

3 tablespoons olive oil

Chop the peppers and beat the eggs with the salt and pepper. Heat the oil in a frying pan and fry the peppers for about 5 minutes. Add the eggs and cook until barely firm.

 SERVES 3

〰〰 CREOLE POACHED EGGS 〰〰

Rice or hot French bread goes with this dish.

1 medium onion, finely chopped
4 tablespoons butter
2 green bell peppers, finely chopped
¼ pound mushrooms, sliced
Coarse salt and freshly ground pepper
1 teaspoon cayenne pepper
1½ cups Chicken Stock (page 42)
2 cups Spicy Tomato Sauce (page 243) (or 2 small cans Italian tomatoes plus juice)
1 teaspoon vinegar
Herb bouquet (parsley, thyme, and bay leaf tied in cheesecloth)
3 cloves
8 eggs
Fresh chopped parsley to garnish

Soften the onion in the butter in a large casserole. Add the peppers and cook for a few minutes, then add the mushrooms, salt, pepper, and cayenne. Cook for a few more minutes, then add the stock, sauce, vinegar, herb bouquet, and cloves. Cover and simmer over very low heat for about 20 minutes. Carefully break in the eggs, one at a time. Cover and poach until the eggs are done. Remove herb bouquet, sprinkle with chopped parsley, and serve.

 SERVES 4

ᗐᐯᐯᐯ CURRY OMELET ᗐᐯᐯᐯ

This is a combination of East-West cooking techniques. The sauce improves if made the night before. Make the omelets in an omelet pan. I prefer to make individual omelets, but if you wish, you can make two large ones and cut them in half.

4 tablespoons *ghee* (page 38) or butter

1 medium onion, finely chopped

1 clove garlic

½ teaspoon turmeric

½ teaspoon ground cumin

½ teaspoon ground coriander

¼ teaspoon ground ginger

2 green fresh chilies, minced (pages 14–16)

A little water

Coarse salt and freshly ground pepper

4 tablespoons cooked chicken, diced

8 eggs

Heat the *ghee* or butter in a saucepan and soften the onion with the garlic. Add the spices and chilies and cook for 2 minutes without burning. Add the water, salt, pepper, and chicken. Cook for 5 minutes. Set aside.

Make the omelets, and just before they are ready (i.e., when they are still runny in the middle) spoon in some of the curry mixture. Fold over and serve at once.

❧ SERVES 4

ᗯᗩᗯ INDIAN SCRAMBLED EGGS ᗯᗩᗯ

Serve these with *Chapattis* (see page 217).

6 eggs
Coarse salt and freshly
   ground pepper
¼ cup milk
3 tablespoons *ghee* (page
   38) or butter
1 medium onion, chopped
1-inch piece of fresh
   ginger, finely chopped
Fresh coriander (a
   handful), chopped
½ teaspoon turmeric
2 teaspoons fresh chilies,
   finely chopped (pages
   13–16)

Beat the eggs in a bowl with salt, pepper, and milk. Heat the *ghee* or butter in a skillet and gently fry the onion with the ginger until soft. Add the coriander, turmeric, and chilies, and fry for another couple of minutes. Pour in the eggs, turn the heat way down, and cook very slowly, stirring. When the eggs are barely set, turn out and serve.

 SERVES 3

SEAFOOD

Some of the best dishes in the world are made from the fish along tropical coastlines. Hot peppers and spices, combined with lemon or lime juice, coconut milk, and fresh ginger, are used to marinate raw fish, which is then either eaten raw or prepared in a variety of ways. The Chinese use sesame oil, hot peppers, garlic, and soy sauce; the Indonesians marinate fish in vinegar, oil, and coconut milk. The Moroccans are extraordinarily inventive with olives and preserved lemons; the Mexicans with capers, chilies, and pimiento-stuffed olives. The Indians prepare fish with a mixture of ground spices (*masala*), the Europeans with mustard and paprika. Many of the superb dishes that distinguish African, Creole, Asian, and Latin American cooking can be duplicated in the American kitchen. Spices should be freshly ground and no substitutes should be used.

Be sure to choose fish that have firm slithery flesh, bright eyes, rosy gills, and no smell. Avoid frozen fish if possible, particularly if there is a deposit of frozen juices at the bottom of the packet. This means it has been thawed and frozen again. Do not use frozen fish for marinated raw dishes.

MARINATED RED SNAPPER,
〰 GHANA-STYLE 〰

This can be served as an appetizer or main course. The snapper must be extremely fresh.

2½ to 3 pounds red snapper, filleted
Juice of 3 lemons
½ cup olive oil
4 fresh chilies, chopped (pages 15–16)
2 tablespoons fresh thyme
2 tablespoons fresh parsley, chopped
Coarse salt and freshly ground pepper
½ cup fresh grated coconut

Slice the fillets into pieces about 2 by 3 inches. Marinate the fish in the lemon juice for 3 hours, or until it has turned opaque. Combine the remaining ingredients and toss the fish in this mixture. Serve chilled.

 **SERVES 4 TO 6**

〜〜 CANGREJOS ENCHILADOS 〜〜

CRABS IN PEPPER SAUCE, DOMINICAN REPUBLIC

Serve with plain boiled rice.

1 pound fresh crabmeat
¼ cup olive oil
1 large onion, chopped
3 cloves garlic, finely
chopped
1 green bell pepper,
chopped
3 hot chilies, finely
chopped (pages 13–16)
6 medium tomatoes,
peeled and chopped
(page 21)
3 tablespoons tomato
purée
½ cup dry sherry
Coarse salt and freshly
ground pepper
2 tablespoons lime juice
2 tablespoons chopped
fresh parsley

Pick over the crabmeat to remove bits of shell or cartilage. In a heavy 12-inch skillet heat the oil. Cook the onion with the garlic, peppers, and chilies until tender. Add the tomatoes, tomato purée, sherry, salt, and pepper, and cook, stirring, for about 10 minutes. Add the lime juice, stir well, then add the crabmeat. Cook over very low heat, covered, for 2 to 3 minutes, just enough to heat the crabmeat. Do not overcook. Correct seasoning. Sprinkle with parsley and serve.

 SERVES 4

SCALLOPS WITH HOT PEPPERS,
〰〰 **GARLIC, AND LINGUINE** 〰〰

The flavor of the scallops in this dish marries well with the spiciness of the sauce and their crispy texture provides a perfect foil for the pasta.

1 pound sea scallops
Juice of half a lemon
1 medium onion, chopped
3 cloves garlic, minced
3 tablespoons olive oil
3 cups canned Italian tomatoes, chopped, with their juice
Coarse salt and freshly ground pepper to taste
½ teaspoon hot pepper flakes (or more to taste)
1 teaspoon fresh rosemary leaves or ½ teaspoon dried
2 to 3 tablespoons unsalted butter, melted
1 cup toasted, fine bread crumbs
10 ounces linguine

Marinate the scallops in the lemon juice for an hour. Meanwhile, soften the onion with the garlic in 2 tablespoons of the olive oil. Add the tomatoes, salt, pepper, hot pepper flakes, and rosemary. Simmer very gently, uncovered, for 20 minutes.

Preheat broiler. Bring 6 quarts water to boil for the linguine.

Dry the scallops with paper towels, dip in the melted butter and the bread crumbs, shaking off any excess. Broil, turning once until lightly browned.

Put the linguine on to cook and cut the scallops into halves or quarters, depending on how large they are. Add to the sauce and keep warm (do not cook or they will be tough).

When the linguine is al dente, drain it and toss in a warmed serving bowl with the remaining tablespoon of olive oil. Top with the scallop sauce.

❧ **SERVES 4**

〰 ESCOVITCH 〰

JAMAICAN MARINATED FISH

3 pounds red snapper, filleted (or any firm-fleshed white fish)
Coarse salt and freshly ground pepper
1 cup olive oil
4 medium onions, thinly sliced
2 bell peppers, cut into strips
2 cloves garlic, peeled
2 bay leaves
½ teaspoon crushed red pepper
¾ cup vinegar
¼ cup water

Cut the fillets into 1½-inch pieces. Season and fry in 2 to 3 tablespoons of the olive oil. Transfer to a shallow serving dish.

Combine the rest of the ingredients (except the olive oil) in a heavy saucepan and simmer until the onion is cooked. Add the remaining oil, mix well, pour the mixture over the fish, and leave it to marinate in the refrigerator for at least a day before serving.

 **SERVES 6 TO 8**

⋙ SZECHUAN SHRIMP ⋙

Rice (see pages 211–212) goes with this peppery shrimp dish. Beer is a good drink with it, and a salad to follow (see Green Salad with Vinaigrette Dressing, page 223) makes it a complete meal.

2 pounds shrimp
2 egg whites
Salt
2 tablespoons cornstarch
Peanut or vegetable oil
for deep frying
2 tablespoons sesame oil
2 cloves garlic, chopped
1-inch piece of fresh
ginger, chopped
3 scallions, chopped
2 teaspoons crushed red
pepper
2 green chili peppers,
diced (pages 14–16)
2 tablespoons dry sherry
1 teaspoon soy sauce
¼ teaspoon sugar
1 tablespoon catsup
½ cup chicken stock
Coarse salt and freshly
ground pepper

Shell and devein the shrimp. Beat the egg whites with a little salt until stiff and mix in the cornstarch. Coat the shrimp with this mixture and let stand for a few hours.

Deep-fry the shrimp in the peanut or vegetable oil, a few at a time in a basket, and drain on paper towels. Meanwhile, heat the sesame oil in a frying pan and stir-fry the garlic, ginger, scallions, red pepper, and chilies. Combine the sherry, soy sauce, sugar, catsup, stock, and seasonings in a bowl. Add the shrimp to the frying pan, pour in the sauce, and bring to a boil. Remove from heat and serve at once.

🌶 SERVES 4

⋁⋀⋁ HUNGARIAN SHRIMP PAPRIKASH ⋁⋀⋁

Plain rice and a green vegetable such as zucchini, peas, broccoli, string beans, or lima beans are good accompaniments here.

3 tablespoons shallots, chopped

4 tablespoons butter

2 pounds shrimp, peeled

Coarse salt and freshly ground pepper

Cayenne to taste

1½ tablespoons Hungarian paprika

½ cup heavy cream

½ cup sour cream

1 tablespoon Dijon mustard

Fresh chopped parsley to garnish

Soften the shallots in the butter and add the shrimp. Cook for a few minutes, until barely turned pink, with the salt, pepper, cayenne, and paprika added. Add the cream, sour cream, and the mustard, and heat through without boiling. Serve immediately, sprinkled with parsley.

 SERVES 4

SHRIMP IN SPICY BLACK BEAN
⌒⌒⌒ **SAUCE WITH ORIENTAL NOODLES** ⌒⌒⌒

Shrimp, salt-leached to make them crisp, are stir-fried and served in a sauce made with chili paste and soy and *hoisin* sauces. The shrimp are served on a bed of thin Oriental wheat noodles scented with sesame oil. Stir-fried Chinese cabbage is a good accompaniment.

2 pounds shrimp, peeled

Coarse salt

6 scallions

2 cloves garlic

4 tablespoons Chinese preserved black beans

1 green chili (pages 14–15)

1 teaspoon cornstarch

2 tablespoons water

2 tablespoons *hoisin* sauce

1 tablespoon chili paste

1 tablespoon soy sauce

½ cup dry white wine, rice wine, chicken stock, or beer

1 pound Oriental wheat noodles

1 tablespoon Oriental sesame oil

4 tablespoons peanut oil

4 tablespoons fresh ginger, minced

Sprigs of fresh coriander to garnish

Place the shrimp in a large bowl and cover with very cold water. Add about 4 tablespoons coarse salt and refrigerate for half an hour. Drain, rinse under cold running water and repeat, refrigerating for another half an hour.

Meanwhile chop the scallions and peel and mince the garlic. Rinse the black beans thoroughly under cold running water and chop fine. Seed and finely chop the chili and set aside.

Combine the cornstarch with the water and mix to a smooth paste. Add the *hoisin* sauce, chili paste, soy sauce, and white wine and mix well. Set aside.

Drain the shrimp and rinse under cold running water. Pat dry with paper towels.

Cook and drain the noodles (they should be al dente). Stir in the sesame oil and place the noodles in a heated serving dish. Keep warm while you cook the shrimp.

Heat the peanut oil in a wok or large frying pan and stir-fry the scallions, garlic, and ginger for 1 to 2 minutes. Add the black beans and chili and stir-fry 1 minute. Add the shrimp and stir-fry until they turn pink, then add the sauce and stir-fry until the shrimp turn opaque (do not overcook them or they will be tough and dry). Turn out the mixture onto the noodles, sprinkle with coriander and serve.

❧ SERVES 4

COD BROCHETTES
WITH MUSTARD SAUCE

Mustard Sauce (pages 238–239)

4 thick cod steaks (about 2 to 2½ pounds)

Coarse salt

Plain white flour

Cayenne pepper

Oil for deep frying

Make the mustard sauce and keep warm in the top of a double boiler. Cut fish into 1-inch squares and thread on small skewers. Salt the fish, flour it, and sprinkle with cayenne. Deep-fry in very hot oil until golden. Serve at once with mustard sauce in a separate bowl.

❧ SERVES 4 TO 6

⋙ INDIAN FRIED FISH ⋙

The flour for the batter may be a combination of 2 tablespoons white flour and 2 tablespoons *besan* (split-pea flour), which can be bought in Indian shops. Ground yellow split peas make a good substitute.

1 pound plaice, sole, or flounder (or any white, filleted fish)

1 teaspoon *Garam Masala* (page 27)

½ teaspoon chili powder

4 tablespoons flour

1 egg

2 tablespoons water

Oil for deep frying

Lemon pickle

Cut the fillets into ⅔-inch strips. Season them with half the *garam masala* and chili powder. Combine the flour, egg, water, and remaining *garam masala* and dip the fish pieces into the mixture. Deep-fry in hot oil until golden. Serve with lemon pickle.

 **SERVES 2 TO 4**

〰〰 FISH STEAKS WITH CHILI SAUCE 〰〰

Fried plantains or bananas (see page 191), Mexican Beans (see page 206), or rice all go with this Latin American dish. A green vegetable and hot French or Italian bread would also be good accompaniments.

Olive oil

2 medium onions, sliced

2 cloves garlic, sliced

4 red or green chili peppers, chopped (pages 13–16)

6 tomatoes, chopped (or a 1-pound can of Italian tomatoes)

1 tablespoon fresh chopped basil

½ teaspoon oregano

Coarse salt and freshly ground pepper

1½ to 2 pounds fish steaks (swordfish, halibut, tilefish, or tuna)

Coat the bottom of a large casserole with olive oil. Place the onions, garlic, and chilies in the oil and cook gently for about 5 minutes. Add the tomatoes, herbs, salt, and pepper. Season the steaks, place them on the mixture, and cover. Cook over medium heat on top of the stove for about 20 minutes. Baste frequently with the sauce and turn the steaks once so that they are fully cooked on both sides.

 SERVES 4

∿∿ AFRICAN STEWED FISH ∿∿

Serve this stew with rice or corn.

4 firm, white fish fillets, cut into pieces 2-inches square
Flour for dredging
Coarse salt and freshly ground pepper
¼ cup peanut oil
2 medium onions, sliced
4 large tomatoes or a 1-pound can of tomatoes
1 teaspoon tomato paste
Crushed red pepper to taste (about 1 tablespoon)
1 cup Fish Stock (pages 42–43)
Fresh chopped basil or parsley

Dredge the fish with seasoned flour. Heat the oil in a casserole and fry the fillets. Remove and drain. Add the onions and chopped tomatoes and cook for 5 minutes. Add the tomato paste, crushed red pepper, and stock. Simmer gently for about 15 minutes. Add the fish and cook for a further 5 minutes. Correct seasoning and serve, sprinkled with chopped basil or parsley.

 SERVES 4

∿∿∿ MOROCCAN RICE-STUFFED FISH ∿∿∿

5 pounds whole fish (red snapper, striped bass, halibut, grouper)

Chermoula **(page 253)**

½ cup rice

2 pounds tomatoes

6 ounces pitted green olives

1 Moroccan Preserved Lemon (page 260)

2 sticks butter

2 green chilies, (pages 14–16)

Coarse salt and freshly ground pepper

Wash and clean the fish; the head and tail should be left on. Leave in the marinade for at least an hour, more if possible.

Parboil the rice for 5 minutes. Peel and seed the tomatoes, dice them, and reserve the juice. Parboil the olives, dice them, dice the preserved lemon peel, and mix with the tomatoes and the *chermoula*. Add the parboiled rice to this mixture.

Put some butter in the inside of the fish, season with salt and pepper, add the *chermoula*-rice mixture, and secure the cavity with a skewer. Cover the fish with remaining butter and chopped chilies. Pour on the reserved tomato juice. Bake, covered, in a preheated 375-degree oven for about 1¼ hours.

 SERVES 6

BAKED WHOLE SEA BASS
◇◇◇ WITH SESAME MARINADE ◇◇◇

1 3-pound sea bass

3 tablespoons *tahini*

2 cloves garlic, peeled

1 green chili, seeded
(pages 14–16)

2 tablespoons peanut or
safflower oil

1 tablespoon soy sauce

2 tablespoons fresh
ginger, minced

Juice of half a lemon, or to
taste

Freshly ground pepper to
taste

2 tablespoons fresh thyme
leaves

6 scallions, sliced

2 tablespoons toasted
sesame seeds

Preheat oven to 375 degrees. Wipe the fish dry with paper towels. Place the *tahini,* garlic, chili, oil, soy sauce, ginger, lemon juice, and pepper in food processor and purée. Mix in the thyme and spread the mixture over the fish, inside and out. Sprinkle with scallions and bake for 45 minutes or until done. Sprinkle with toasted sesame seeds and serve.

 SERVES 4

MOROCCAN FISH
ᗯᗯ WITH TOMATOES AND FENNEL ᗯᗯ

Moroccans cook fish in a *tajin*, an earthenware pot with a conical lid, in which they lay pieces of cane to keep the fish from touching the bottom and burning. Carrots, celery, and fennel can also be used for this, and the latter adds a delicious aroma to the fish. Use a heavy casserole and either bake this in the oven or cook it on the top of the stove.

**4½ to 5 pounds fish
(striped bass, red
snapper, etc., left whole
if small, or cut into
steaks)**
***Chermoula* (page 253)**
3 pounds tomatoes
1 teaspoon ground ginger
1 pinch pulverized saffron
2 cloves garlic, chopped
**½ teaspoon dried ground
chilies (pages 13–16)**
2 tablespoons olive oil
**Coarse salt and freshly
ground pepper**
**1 Moroccan Preserved
Lemon (page 260)**
6 green olives, pitted
**3 heads fennel, sliced,
leaves reserved**
**Fresh chopped coriander
to garnish**

Wash the fish, pat it dry, and marinate for at least an hour in the *chermoula*. Peel and seed the tomatoes and put them, with their juice, in a saucepan. Add the ginger, saffron, garlic, chili, olive oil, salt, and pepper, and simmer gently, stirring frequently, until you have a thick purée. Add the preserved lemon and olives and set aside.

Arrange the fennel slices across the bottom of a *tajin* or heavy casserole. Place the fish on the fennel and pour on the remaining *chermoula* and the tomato purée. Cook on the top of the stove over medium-low heat for 30 minutes, or bake for 45 minutes at 350 degrees. Garnish with coriander and chopped fennel leaves and serve hot or cold.

 SERVES 6

∿∿ DEEP-FRIED FISH SZECHUAN ∿∿

Use a firm-fleshed white fish (bass, halibut, etc.). Rice (see pages 211–212) and a green vegetable are the best accompaniments.

2 pounds fish fillets

1 egg

6 tablespoons sherry

5 tablespoons flour

Coarse salt and freshly ground pepper

Peanut or vegetable oil for deep frying

2 tablespoons sesame oil

1 cup bamboo shoots, chopped (or 1 small can)

1 green chili, minced (pages 14–16)

1 scallion, chopped

½-inch piece of fresh ginger, chopped

1 teaspoon vinegar

3 tablespoons soy sauce

1 cup Fish or Chicken Stock (pages 42–43)

1 tablespoon cornstarch mixed to a paste with 1 tablespoon cold water

Cut the fish into 2-inch squares. Mix the egg with 4 tablespoons of the sherry, flour, salt, and pepper. Dip the fish fillets into this batter and deep-fry. Drain on paper towels.

Meanwhile heat the sesame oil in a frying pan and stir-fry the bamboo shoots, chili, scallion, and ginger. Add the vinegar and soy sauce. Cook for 2 minutes, then add the fish with the stock and remaining 2 tablespoons of sherry. Bring to boil, add the cornstarch mixture, and cook for 2 minutes. Correct seasoning and serve.

 SERVES 4

〰️ BALINESE SPICED FISH 〰️

Serve with rice.

1 3- to 4-pound whole
   fish (snapper, striped
   bass, any firm,
   white-fleshed fish)
1 teaspoon crushed chili
   peppers
Juice of 1 lemon
¼ teaspoon ground
   allspice
2 cloves garlic, minced
2 tablespoons chopped
   fresh ginger
2 tablespoons soy sauce
3 scallions, including
   green part, chopped
½ cup peanut or
   vegetable oil
Coarse salt and freshly
   ground pepper

Pat the fish dry with paper towels. Mix together all the remaining ingredients and coat the fish with the mixture, inside and out. Leave for at least an hour at room temperature.

Preheat oven to 375 degrees. Bake, covered, until done (about half an hour), turning once.

🌭 SERVES 4

SALMON WITH
∿∿∿ TARRAGON-MUSTARD SAUCE ∿∿∿

Nothing wakes up the palate and perks up the flavor in food like a touch of mustard. But more often we think of it as something to be spread on a hamburger or added to a salad dressing than to be used for cooking. I like to mix it with oil and brush it lightly over fish fillets before broiling them. I also add it to marinade for lamb or pork chops or mix it in with cream sauces, which it helps to thicken. It is excellent with rather bland meats such as rabbit or chicken, and particularly good with the delicate taste of veal kidneys.

The best mustard for cooking comes from Dijon in Burgundy, where half the world's mustard is made. This mustard is a smooth, hot, grayish yellow paste consisting of ground, hulled mustard seeds mixed with white wine, vinegar or *verjuice* (the juice of green grapes) and spices. By law, no fortifiers, such as mustard oil, flour fillers, or sugar are allowed in Dijon mustards. Grey Poupon Dijon mustard, which can be found in most supermarkets, is made in America, using the original French recipe. It is not as fine as its French counterpart, but it is inexpensive and perfectly good.

The following dish, in which broiled salmon is served with a light tarragon-mustard sauce made with cream and white wine, is especially good with new potatoes and asparagus.

FISH

4 salmon steaks or 2 fillets (about 2 pounds)
Juice of half a lemon or lime
1 tablespoon peanut or vegetable oil

Sprinkle the steaks or fillets with the lemon juice and the oil. Set aside. Preheat broiler.

Soften the shallots in 1 tablespoon of the butter in a small saucepan. Add the white wine and fish stock and reduce to ¾ cup (about 10 minutes).

SAUCE

2 shallots, minced

2 tablespoons unsalted butter

1 cup dry white wine

1 cup fish stock or bottled clam juice

2 tablespoons minced fresh tarragon leaves

1 tablespoon Dijon mustard

½ cup heavy cream

Coarse salt and freshly ground pepper to taste

Turn heat down to low and add the tarragon leaves and the mustard. Stir well and add the heavy cream.

Broil the fish until cooked (about 3 to 5 minutes on each side, depending on thickness).

Right before serving, stir remaining butter into the sauce and season to taste with salt and pepper. Pass the sauce separately in a heated bowl at the table.

SERVES 4

NOTE: Serve with new potatoes.

⋀⋁⋀⋁ MACKEREL WITH MUSTARD SAUCE ⋀⋁⋀⋁

A green vegetable and rice go well with this dish.

FISH

**4 small or 2 large
  mackerel**
Juice of 1 lemon
**Coarse salt and freshly
  ground pepper**
2 tablespoons olive oil

SAUCE

**3 tablespoons shallots or
  scallions, chopped**
3 tablespoons butter
1 teaspoon flour
½ cup dry white wine
**4 tablespoons Dijon or
  dark mustard**
Fresh chopped parsley

Clean the mackerel and squeeze the lemon juice into the cavities. Season, sprinkle with oil, and broil for about 5 minutes on each side.

Meanwhile cook the shallots in the butter without browning. Add the flour and cook for 2 minutes. Add the wine and mustard and stir thoroughly. Bring to a boil, stirring, and cook until thickened. Remove from heat, pour over the mackerel, and sprinkle with parsley.

 SERVES 4

⌁ INDONESIAN SPICED MACKEREL ⌁

Serve this with rice and grilled or stewed tomatoes.

1 medium onion, chopped
¾ cup water
4 tablespoons fresh green chili, chopped (pages 14–16)
½-inch piece of fresh ginger, diced
2 cloves garlic, chopped
Coarse salt and freshly ground pepper to taste
Peanut or vegetable oil
4 small or 2 large mackerel
About 1 tablespoon red wine vinegar
2 tablespoons fresh chopped basil

Combine the onion, water, chili, ginger, and garlic in a blender and purée. Heat about 3 tablespoons peanut oil in a skillet and fry the mixture over high heat, stirring constantly. Correct seasoning and keep warm.

Clean the mackerel and put a little vinegar and basil in the cavities. Sprinkle with peanut oil and grill under a broiler.

When ready to serve, spoon the sauce over the mackerel.

 SERVES 4

RED SNAPPER WITH
∿∿∿ HAZELNUT-PEPPER VINAIGRETTE ∿∿∿

Hazelnut oil is most often used in salads, but its rich toasted flavor also goes beautifully with fish. The sweet succulent flesh of red snapper, bass, or trout or fish steaks such as halibut, swordfish, or tilefish is a perfect foil for the fragrant, nutty taste of the oil— especially when fresh herbs such as tarragon, thyme, or basil are added.

A whole red snapper or sea bass is delicious served with a vinaigrette made from hazelnut oil, limes, *tomatillos,* toasted peppers, chilies, and fresh coriander. The sauce and the fish can be served hot or cold, making the dish particularly good for a lunch or dinner party. *Couscous* or toasted *polenta* squares go very well with this dish.

Because hazelnut oil breaks down quickly over heat, it is generally added at the end of cooking. It spoils quickly in warm weather and should always be refrigerated. If it turns cloudy after a spell in the refrigerator, there will be no adverse effect on the flavor. When a jar of oil is opened, it should smell mildly and pleasantly fragrant. Rancid oil will have an unmistakable, bitter, metallic taste.

For salads, hazelnut oil goes especially well with sherry vinegar. It is good on delicate greens such as Boston or bibb lettuce. Instead of vinegar, lemon juice can be used.

An added bonus in using hazelnut oil is that it is polyunsaturated, as are the oils in fish. So it makes for a nutritious and low-fat meal.

Tomatillos, cousins of the cape gooseberry, are sold fresh or canned. Fresh ones have a papery wrapping that should be removed before they are used.

FISH

1 3- to 4-pound red
    snapper
1 tablespoon hazelnut oil
Juice of half a lime

VINAIGRETTE

1 red bell pepper
1 yellow bell pepper
4 *tomatillos*
2 *jalapeño* chilies, seeded
    and minced (pages
    14–16)
1 clove garlic, minced
½ small red onion, finely
    chopped
½ cup hazelnut oil
Juice of half a lime
4 tablespoons fresh
    coriander, chopped
Coarse salt and freshly
    ground pepper to taste

To prepare the fish, first wipe the snapper inside and out with paper towels. Sprinkle it with about a tablespoon of hazelnut oil and the lime juice. Set aside.

To prepare the vinaigrette, first preheat the broiler. Seed the peppers and cut them into quarters. Place them skin-side up on a grilling rack and broil until their skins are charred. Place them in a plastic or paper bag and let them cool. Peel off the skins.

Meanwhile quarter the *tomatillos* and simmer them in water to cover until soft. Drain and chop. Chop the peppers.

Place the *tomatillos,* peppers, chilies, garlic, and onion in a small bowl. Add the hazelnut oil and toss thoroughly. Add the lime juice to taste.

Just before serving, stir in the coriander and season with salt and pepper to taste.

Broil the snapper for about 7 minutes on each side or until cooked. Pass the vinaigrette separately.

✽ **SERVES 4**

⌇⌇⌇ RED SNAPPER VERACRUZ ⌇⌇⌇

Mexican Beans (see page 206) are good with this dish, as is rice.

**1 3- to 4-pound red
snapper, head on**
Juice of 1 lime or lemon
**Coarse salt and freshly
ground black pepper**
½ cup olive oil
1 medium onion, chopped
2 cloves garlic, chopped
¾ cup tomato purée
**5 tomatoes, peeled and
chopped (page 21)**
**4 *jalapeño* chilies, fresh or
canned, chopped (pages
14–16)**
**¼ teaspoon ground
cinnamon**
¼ teaspoon ground cloves
2 teaspoons capers
1 cup fish stock or water
**Sliced pimiento-stuffed
olives to garnish**

Rub the fish inside and out with the lemon juice and season. Heat the oil in a skillet and soften the onion with the garlic. Add the tomato purée, tomatoes, chilies, cinnamon, cloves, capers, and stock. Bring to a boil, turn down, and simmer gently for 10 minutes.

Put some sauce on the bottom of a poaching dish, place the fish on top, and cover with the remaining sauce. Simmer until cooked. Remove to a heated dish, spoon the sauce over the fish, and decorate with the olives.

 **SERVES 4 TO 6**

ᗦᐯᐯ JAMAICAN FISH CAKES ᐯᐯᗝ

These fish cakes make a good cheap meal; they are filling and nutritious. Accompany them with a green vegetable, such as spinach, broccoli, or zucchini, and rice, if you like.

Salt cod must be soaked overnight in several changes of water. I rinse it thoroughly each time. You can test its final saltiness by licking it. If it is not too salty after the final rinsing, I suggest cooking it in the milk instead of water and reserving the milk to use in the batter, cooling it first. If the fish is very salty, cook it in water (which you throw out) and don't salt the fish cakes.

½ pound salt cod

Water or milk to cover

2 tablespoons *Achiote* Oil (page 34)

2 medium onions, chopped

1 cup flour

1 teaspoon baking powder

Coarse salt and freshly ground pepper

¾ cup milk

1 egg

1 tablespoon melted butter

2 small chilies, finely chopped

Simmer the fish for 20 minutes in water or milk to cover until it flakes with a fork. Remove from heat and set aside. Heat the oil and fry the onions over low heat until soft. Set aside.

Sift the flour into a bowl with the baking powder and seasonings. Make a well in the middle and add the milk and beaten egg. Add the butter and mix well. Add the chilies, onions, and fish and mix thoroughly. Fry a table-spoon of the batter at a time in oil in a skillet for about 2 minutes on each side. Remove to drain on paper towels and serve.

 SERVES 4

ᗺᗺᗺ PAELLA ᗺᗺᗺ

There are hundreds of versions of paella, and no two Spaniards are likely to agree on the ingredients. One thing is essential, however: A true paella must be made with Valencia rice, which is short and stubby, if the paella is to have the right consistency (California pearl rice or arborio rice may also be used). The rice should be firm, not mushy or watery. Paella should be made in a flat metal pan that has handles on both sides. If you do not own a paella pan, use a frying pan with a wide flat base, about 2 inches deep and 12 inches across, that will go into the oven.

About 2 pints Chicken Stock (page 42)

½ teaspoon saffron threads

1 2- to 3-pound chicken, cut up into 8 pieces

2 tablespoons olive oil

4 *chorizos,* sliced

1 medium onion, chopped

2 cloves garlic, minced

3 pimientos, chopped

1 pound medium shrimp, shelled

2 cups short-grain rice

½ pound fresh or frozen peas

Juice of half a lemon

Coarse salt and freshly ground pepper to taste

Simmer the stock with the saffron threads for 15 minutes. Set aside.

Meanwhile, dry the chicken pieces with paper towels and brown them lightly in the olive oil a few at a time. Remove and set aside. Add the *chorizos* and brown lightly. Add the onion, garlic, and pimientos and sauté until the onion is soft. Add the shrimp and cook for 1 to 2 minutes. Remove the shrimp and set aside.

Preheat oven to 325 degrees.

Add the rice to the pan and stir thoroughly with a wooden spoon to coat with the oil. Meanwhile, bring the chicken stock to simmer and add it to the rice, reserving about ¼ cup

**1 pound mussels,
scrubbed, debearded,
and thoroughly rinsed
Fresh chopped parsley to
garnish**

of stock to cook the mussels in later. Add the peas, lemon juice, salt and pepper and cook over high heat for 10 minutes.

Place the chicken in the rice and bake for 15 minutes in the oven. Add the shrimp and continue baking until all the liquid is evaporated from the rice (about 20 minutes). Meanwhile, toss the mussels in the reserved stock (there should be enough to cover the bottom of the pan) for a few minutes until the shells have opened. Discard those that do not open during cooking. Add the mussels to the paella when it has cooked. Decorate the paella with parsley and serve.

SERVES 4 TO 6

ᗡᐯᐯᐯ KEDGEREE ᐯᐯᐯᗡ

This dish originated in India and became extremely popular in England, where it is often made from smoked haddock. Other suitable fish include any white fish and salmon. This is my own version, a combination of Indian and British.

½ **pound long-grain rice**

1 medium onion, chopped

1 stick butter

2 fresh chilies, cut in thin strips (pages 13–16)

2 tablespoons fresh ginger, minced

¼ **teaspoon turmeric**

1 tablespoon Mild Curry Powder (page 26)

1 pound cooked smoked haddock

4 hard-boiled eggs, diced

Coarse salt and freshly ground pepper

2 to 3 tablespoons heavy cream

2 tablespoons chopped fresh parsley

Boil the rice until cooked and drain (see pages 211–212). Soften the onion in the butter without browning, add the chilies and ginger, and cook for 2 minutes. Add the turmeric and curry powder and cook 2 more minutes. Add the fish and hard-boiled eggs. Mix and heat through. Add the cooked rice and stir with a fork. Season to taste with salt and pepper. Stir in the cream just before serving and sprinkle with parsley.

 **SERVES 4 TO 6**

POULTRY

There was a time when chicken was a luxury, but now it is one of the cheapest meats on the market. Unfortunately, the free-range bird, which was so delicious when roasted simply with butter and tarragon, has been replaced by the factory-raised hen, whose value is calculated down to the last minute of its life. Modern chickens never see the light of day; their feet never touch the ground. They sit immobilized in cages too small to turn in, where they are fed with artificial feeds and injected with hormones. Quite apart from the discouraging humanitarian aspect of this treatment, they offer little in terms of taste. Spices and aromatics have become essential if such chickens are to be palatable. Turmeric, saffron, paprika, and chilies give rich color and flavor to an otherwise dull bird.

Fresh chicken should have white, firm skin and no unpleasant smell. Check packaged chicken to make sure there is no deposit of frozen juices at the bottom. This means it has been frozen and thawed. Frozen poultry is often tough because it is put in the freezer too soon after it has been slaughtered. The best chicken comes from a good butcher or from a farmer who still raises free-range birds.

CHICKEN WITH ANCHO
〰〰 **CHILIES AND GRILLED POLENTA** 〰〰

Chicken marinated in a paste made from *ancho* chilies develops a deep full flavor and the sauce can be mopped up with triangles of *polenta,* grilled so that they are crisp on the outside and creamy in the center. A sautéed vegetable such as spinach or broccoli rabe (a bitter, leafy cousin of broccoli) goes with this dish.

CHICKEN
4 *ancho* chilies (page 13)
1 3- to 4-pound chicken cut into 8 pieces
Juice of 1 lime
4 tablespoons peanut or vegetable oil
1 large onion
2 large cloves garlic, in their skins
1 teaspoon cayenne pepper
½ teaspoon ground cumin
1 teaspoon fresh thyme leaves (or ½ teaspoon dried)
Coarse salt and freshly ground pepper to taste
½ cup water

POLENTA
3 cups instant *polenta*
2 tablespoons olive oil

To prepare chicken, begin an hour ahead of cooking. Using rubber gloves to protect your hands from the volatile oils, remove the stems and seeds from the chilies and tear the chilies into small strips. Place in a bowl and cover with warm water. Let sit for 30 minutes.

Remove the skin from the chicken pieces and discard. Place the pieces in a large bowl and squeeze the lime juice over them. Place in the refrigerator.

Place the chili pieces in a food processor and add 2 tablespoons of the peanut or vegetable oil and enough of the soaking water to make a smooth purée. Coat the chicken pieces with this mixture and marinate them in the refrigerator for at least 1 hour.

Heat the remaining peanut or vegetable oil in a casserole and soften the onion. Meanwhile simmer the garlic cloves in their skins in water to cover for 10 minutes. Drain, skin, and mash the garlic with a fork. Add it to the onion along with the cayenne pepper and cumin. Cook for 2 to 3 minutes, stirring, then add the chicken pieces with their marinade and the thyme. Season to taste with salt and pepper and add the water. Mix well, cover and simmer for 30 minutes or until chicken is cooked. If the sauce gets too dry add a little more water. If it is too liquid, uncover and turn up heat until it boils down and thickens.

Make the *polenta* triangles while the chicken is cooking. Preheat broiler. Cook the *polenta* in water according to directions on package (it will take about 5 minutes), adding salt to taste, and pour it out onto a flat surface (a large flat baking sheet will do). Smooth with a spoon and cool. Cut into triangles and place on a broiling sheet.

Brush the *polenta* triangles with the olive oil and broil until the outside is browned and crisp but the inside is still soft and creamy (about 15 to 20 minutes). Arrange the triangles on serving platter and pass chicken and *polenta* separately. Do not turn over.

❧ **SERVES 4**

〰〰 **POULET DIJONNAIS** 〰〰

A French dish, this goes well with rice and a green vegetable.

1 3- to 4-pound chicken
Fresh tarragon (if
available—no substitute)
2 tablespoons Dijon
mustard
2 tablespoons softened
butter
Coarse salt and freshly
ground white pepper
¼ cup brandy
½ cup heavy cream

Wipe the chicken with paper towels and put small pieces of tarragon under the skin. Combine the mustard and the butter and spread it over the chicken, putting a little of the mixture in the cavity. Season with salt and pepper and place in a roasting pan.

Roast in preheated 350-degree oven for about an hour, or until done. Remove to a plate and put the roasting pan on top of the stove. Degrease the pan, bring the cooking juices to a boil, and add the brandy. Cook, stirring, for a minute or so, then add the cream. Heat through, correct seasoning, add more chopped tarragon, and pass the sauce separately in a sauce boat.

 SERVES 4

BAKED CHICKEN
ᗢᗢᗢ WITH MUSTARD SAUCE ᗢᗢᗢ

**1 3- to 4-pound chicken,
cut up**

Flour for dredging

**2 tablespoons unsalted
butter**

**2 tablespoons peanut or
vegetable oil**

¾ cup Dijon mustard

**2 leeks, sliced and
thoroughly washed**

**¼ pound *shiitake*
mushrooms, coarsely
chopped**

**1 tablespoon fresh thyme
leaves**

1 cup heavy cream

¼ cup dry white wine

**Coarse salt and freshly
ground pepper to taste**

Preheat oven to 375 degrees. Skin the chicken pieces and lightly dredge them with the flour. Heat 1 tablespoon of the butter and the oil in a large skillet and gently brown the chicken pieces, a few at a time, on all sides. Remove and, when cool enough to handle, spread all over with the mustard.

Add the leeks to the skillet and cook until soft. Place the leeks over the bottom of a baking dish large enough to hold the chicken in one layer. Arrange the chicken pieces on top.

Melt the remaining tablespoon butter in the skillet and quickly sauté the mushrooms. Add them to the chicken. Sprinkle with thyme and pour on the cream and wine. Season to taste with salt and pepper.

Cover loosely with foil and bake for 20 minutes. Remove foil and continue to bake until the chicken is tender and the sauce has thickened. Correct seasoning and serve.

 **SERVES 4 TO 6**

ROAST CHICKEN WITH
〰〰 COUSCOUS AND HARISSA SAUCE 〰〰

Pigeon stuffed with *couscous* and roasted is a popular Morccoan dish. Chicken is also good cooked this way, especially when the *couscous* is flavored with tarragon and roasted red peppers. This dish is good hot or cold and can be served with sautéed spinach or salad and *Harissa* Sauce (see page 265). You can also buy the sauce.

If you "air dry" a chicken before cooking it, it will have a silky taut skin. Leave the chicken overnight or for a couple of hours unwrapped on rack in the refrigerator with a plate underneath to catch any juices. The air will circulate around it and dry out the skin.

Roast the chicken first on one side, then the other, finishing it breast up. This will make for juicier breast meat and allow the skin to be browned. Always let the chicken rest before carving it to give the juices time to develop. If possible let it rest for an hour—chicken needn't be piping hot—the difference is remarkable.

1 3- to 4-pound chicken
Juice of half a lemon
1 red pepper
2 large shallots, finely chopped
1 small clove garlic, minced
2 tablespoons unsalted butter
1 cup instant *couscous*
1 cup boiling water
Pinch saffron
Coarse salt and freshly ground pepper

Preheat oven to 400 degrees and preheat broiler.

Wipe the chicken dry with paper towels. Squeeze the lemon juice over the chicken inside and out and set the chicken aside.

Cut the pepper into quarters. Flatten the quarters out and place skin-side up on a broiling rack. Char under the broiler and place in a plastic or paper bag. Cool, skin, and chop.

Meanwhile, soften the shallots and garlic in 1 tablespoon of the butter.

1 tablespoon chopped fresh tarragon or thyme leaves

***Harissa* Sauce (page 265)**

Add the *couscous* and stir thoroughly. Pour in the boiling water, fluff with a fork, and let sit for 5 minutes. Add the saffron and red pepper and season to taste with salt and pepper.

Season the chicken cavity and stuff with the *couscous* mixture. Truss and place the chicken on its side on a roasting rack. Roast for 20 minutes, then turn over and roast on the other side. Finish breast-side up for another 20 minutes or until the juices run yellow when the skin is pricked with a fork. Let rest for at least 10 minutes before serving. Serve the *Harissa* Sauce separately.

SERVES 4

〜〜 DEVILED CHICKEN LEGS 〜〜

Serve these with a piquant mayonnaise. A green vegetable such as broccoli, peas, or braised celery would go well with them.

4 chicken legs, skinned

Melted butter

1 cup fine bread crumbs

1 teaspoon dry mustard

1 teaspoon Mild Curry Powder (page 26)

1 teaspoon cayenne

Coarse salt and freshly ground pepper

Score the flesh on the skinned chicken legs. Dip into melted butter, then into the bread crumbs seasoned with remaining ingredients. Arrange on broiling pan and cook under a hot broiler for about 20 minutes. Occasionally turn the chicken and baste with more melted butter as you go.

 SERVES 4

MOROCCAN CHICKEN
ᴡᴡ WITH LEMON AND OLIVES ᴡᴡ

2 chickens, cut up, with
   livers
Coarse salt and freshly
   ground pepper
1 teaspoon ground ginger
2 tablespoons olive oil
4 tablespoons butter
1 medium onion, cut in
   half
2 cloves garlic, peeled
¼ teaspoon pulverized
   saffron
8 sprigs coriander, tied
   together
2½ cups water
1 Moroccan Preserved
   Lemon (page 260)
10 reddish brown olives
   (use Greek *Kalamatas*
   or Italian *Gaetas*)

Put the chicken and livers in a heavy casserole. Salt and pepper to taste; add ginger, oil, butter, onion, garlic, saffron, coriander, and water. Bring to a boil and simmer gently, partially covered, for about 30 minutes, basting often.

Remove chicken and keep warm. Put the livers, garlic, and onion in blender and reduce to a purée. Return to the casserole with the quartered preserved lemon peel and olives. Bring to a boil and when thick pour over the chicken.

 SERVES 6

◊◊◊ MOROCCAN STEAMED CHICKEN ◊◊◊

2 3-pound chickens

10 small white onions

½ cup chopped parsley

1 stick butter, softened

¼ teaspoon pulverized
 saffron

Coarse salt

Ground cumin

¼ teaspoon dried ground
 chilies (pages 13–16)
 (optional)

Dry the chickens thoroughly with paper towels. Parboil the onions in their skins and peel them. Fill the cavities of the chickens with the onions, parsley, and half the butter. Pound saffron with remaining butter and salt and rub into the skins. Bring water in steamer or *couscoussière* to boil. Arrange chickens in top and cover with cheesecloth. Steam about 1 hour, without lifting the lid.

Serve with bowls of cumin (mixed with chilies if you like) and coarse salt.

 SERVES 6

DJEJ M'HAMMER

MOROCCAN FRIED CHICKEN

2 chickens, whole, with
  livers
Coarse salt and freshly
  ground pepper
2 cloves garlic, peeled
1 medium onion,
  quartered
¼ teaspoon pulverized
  saffron
1 tablespoon paprika
1 teaspoon ground cumin
¼ teaspoon turmeric
1 stick butter
Bunch fresh coriander
2 cups water
1 tablespoon olive oil

Put the chickens in a heavy pan with the livers. Add salt, pepper, garlic, onion, spices, half of the butter, and coriander. Add water and simmer 1 hour, basting frequently. Remove chickens.

Mash the onion in blender with livers and garlic and return to sauce. Set over high heat to reduce.

Meanwhile heat remaining butter and oil in frying pan. Brown the chickens.

Arrange in serving dish and pour the sauce on top. Serve immediately.

 SERVES 6

⋁⋀⋁ DJEJ MECHOUI ⋁⋀⋁

CHARCOAL-BROILED CHICKEN, MOROCCAN-STYLE

4 scallions, white part only

2 cloves garlic, peeled

Coarse salt and freshly ground pepper

2 tablespoons chopped fresh coriander

1½ teaspoons paprika

1 teaspoon ground cumin

¼ teaspoon dried ground chilies (pages 13–16)

1 stick butter, softened

2 broiling chickens, cut in quarters

With a mortar and pestle mash the scallions, garlic, salt, pepper, coriander, paprika, cumin, and chilies with the butter until you have a smooth paste. Cover the chickens with the mixture and set aside for a couple of hours.

Heat charcoal or broiler. Arrange the chickens skin side toward heat and baste until done, turning once.

 SERVES 4

∿∿ DJEJ KDRAS ∿∿

MOROCCAN CHICKEN WITH CHICK-PEAS

This is a Moroccan stew in which the chicken is cooked with *smen*, a strong Moroccan butter, together with onions, paprika, and saffron, with lemon juice squeezed on at the end. Ordinary butter will do as a substitute.

**½ cup dried chick-peas,
  cooked, or 10-ounce can**
2 chickens
**½ teaspoon pulverized
  saffron**
**Coarse salt and freshly
  ground pepper**
3 medium onions, sliced
3-inch cinnamon stick
2½ cups water
**Parsley sprigs, tied
  together**
1 stick butter
Juice of 1 lemon
**2 tablespoons chopped
  fresh coriander**

Soak the dried chick-peas overnight, drain, and simmer them in fresh water for an hour. Drain and peel. Put the chickens and chick-peas into a heavy casserole. (If using canned chick-peas do not add until chickens are cooked.) Add half the saffron, salt and pepper, 1 onion, cinnamon stick, water, parsley, and butter. Simmer for 30 minutes.

Add remaining onions and saffron. Cook 30 minutes more. (Add canned chick-peas at this point.) Remove chickens. Reduce sauce, add lemon juice, correct seasoning, pour over the chickens, sprinkle with coriander and serve.

 **SERVES 4 TO 6**

KOREAN STEWED CHICKEN

2 2½-pound chickens
¾ cup sesame oil
½ cup soy sauce
(preferably tamari)
4 scallions, chopped
3 cloves garlic, minced
2 to 3 tablespoons Korean
red pepper or chili
powder
Coarse salt to taste

Cut the chickens into pieces. Combine remaining ingredients and pour sauce over the chicken, coating the pieces well. Leave to marinate for at least 2 hours, overnight if possible.

Put the chicken and the sauce in a heavy casserole and simmer gently on top of the stove for 1 hour, turning occasionally. Do not add any liquid—there will be a sufficient amount.

❧ **SERVES 6**

〰〰 POLLO EN MOLE VERDE 〰〰

MEXICAN CHICKEN IN GREEN MOLE SAUCE

CHICKEN

2 2½-pound chickens

3 cups water

1 medium onion

1 carrot

SAUCE

4 *poblano* chilies, fresh or
  canned (pages 15–16)

½ cup *pepitas* (pumpkin
  seeds)

½ cup walnuts

½ cup almonds

1 pound *tomatillos* or 2
  10-ounce cans Mexican
  green tomatoes, drained

½ cup fresh coriander,
  chopped

1 clove garlic, peeled

Coarse salt and freshly
  ground pepper

2 tablespoons peanut or
  vegetable oil

To cook the chickens, simmer them in the water with the onion and carrot for about 30 minutes. Drain and reserve the stock.

To cook the sauce, prepare the chilies and combine in a blender with the *pepitas*, walnuts, almonds, *tomatillos*, coriander, and garlic. Blend to a smooth purée and season with salt and pepper.

Heat the oil in a large pan and add the sauce. Bring to a boil and add enough of the cooking liquid from the chickens to make the sauce the consistency of heavy cream. Cook for 20 minutes. Cut the chickens into pieces and add to the sauce. Heat through and serve.

 SERVES 6

ᗯᐯᐯᐯ CHICKEN IN CHILI-WALNUT SAUCE ᗯᐯᐯᐯ

1 3- to 4-pound chicken,
   cut up
Water to cover
5 fresh green chilies
   (pages 14–16)
2 tablespoons peanut,
   sesame, or vegetable oil
4 ounces shelled walnuts
4 ounces shelled peanuts
2 slices bread, crusts
   removed
2 medium onions, peeled
   and coarsely sliced
2 cloves garlic, peeled
2 thick slices of fresh
   ginger
½ teaspoon ground mace
½ teaspoon ground
   cinnamon
2 cloves
Coarse salt and freshly
   ground pepper to taste
Sesame seeds to garnish
Coriander or parsley to
   garnish

Simmer the chicken in water until almost done. Drain and cool, reserving liquid. Toast the chilies, wrap in paper towels, and set aside. In the oil, fry the walnuts, peanuts, and bread until lightly browned. Combine in a blender with the chilies, onions, garlic, ginger, spices, salt, and pepper. Add a cup of the chicken broth and purée.

Thin the mixture with 2 cups of broth and return to pan. Bring to a boil. Add chicken and simmer for about 20 minutes, until thick. Sprinkle with sesame seeds and fresh chopped coriander or parsley and serve.

 SERVES 4

〰️ NEWBURG SAUCE 〰️

Serve this old-fashioned fifties dish with cooked lobster, crab, prawns, or scallops.

3 tablespoons butter
3 tablespoons white flour
1 teaspoon Hungarian paprika
2 cups light cream
3 egg yolks, beaten
1 tablespoon dry sherry
Coarse salt and freshly ground white pepper

Melt the butter in a saucepan. Add the flour and cook for a couple of minutes, taking care to prevent burning. Add the paprika, cook for a minute, then add the cream. Bring to a boil, stirring, and turn down heat. Beat in the egg yolks, taking great care not to maintain too high a heat or they will curdle. Add the sherry, season with salt and pepper, and use either as a separate sauce or add the shellfish to the sauce and heat through.

 **YIELD: ABOUT 1½ CUPS**

∿∿ **HORSERADISH SAUCE** ∿∿

Serve this sauce with boiled or corned beef. It is a popular sauce in Russian and Viennese cooking.

4 tablespoons butter

1 medium onion, finely chopped

4 tablespoons flour

½ cup grated fresh horseradish

2 cups beef or chicken stock

Coarse salt and freshly ground white pepper

1 teaspoon sugar

½ cup sour cream or heavy cream

Melt the butter in a heavy-bottomed saucepan. Fry the onion gently without browning it. Stir in the flour and cook for a few minutes without browning. Add the horseradish, stir in, then add the stock, salt, pepper, and sugar. Beat with a wire whisk until the sauce becomes thick and smooth. Stir in the cream, heat through (without boiling), correct seasoning, and serve.

 **YIELD: ABOUT 2 CUPS**

∿∿∿ CHICKEN WITH MACADAMIA NUTS ∿∿∿

6 macadamia nuts

1 teaspoon coriander seed

¼ teaspoon turmeric

2 cloves garlic, minced

1½ medium onions,
    chopped

2 *serrano* chilies, chopped
    (page 15)

2 tablespoons peanut oil

1 3-pound chicken, cut up

3 cups Coconut Milk
    (pages 36–37)

2 tablespoons chopped
    lemon rind

2 tablespoons soy sauce
    or *ketjap manis* (page 9)

1 tablespoon brown sugar

Coarse salt and freshly
    ground pepper

Grind the nuts, coriander, and turmeric in a spice grinder or with a mortar and pestle. Set aside. Mash the garlic, onions, and chilies to a fine paste either in a blender or with mortar and pestle. Set aside.

Heat the oil in a deep, heavy-bottomed skillet and fry the chicken until lightly browned. Set aside. Fry the spices for 2 to 3 minutes, stirring to prevent burning. Add the onion mixture and cook 5 minutes, without browning. Add the coconut milk, lemon rind, soy sauce or *ketjap manis,* sugar, salt, and pepper and bring to a boil. Return the chicken pieces to the pan (with any juices that might have run out) and simmer, covered, for 20 to 30 minutes, or until chicken is tender.

 SERVES 4

∿∿∿ AJÍ DE GALLINA ∿∿∿

PERUVIAN CHICKEN WITH CHILIES

Its bright colors and attractive patterns make this dish especially good for entertaining. It can be made in advance and heated through.

A salad is all you need to go with it. See page 223 for Green Salad with Vinaigrette Dressing.

1 4-pound chicken, cut up
Water to cover
1 stalk celery with leaves, chopped
3 medium onions, chopped
2 carrots, chopped
8 slices fresh homemade-type white bread
2 cups milk
⅔ cup oil
2 cloves garlic, chopped
2 tablespoons dried red chilies
1 tablespoon *achiote* seeds (page 34)
1 cup walnuts
Coarse salt and freshly ground black pepper
⅓ cup freshly grated Parmesan cheese

Simmer the chicken in the water with the celery, 1 onion, and carrots for about half an hour. Drain and reserve stock for another use. Skin, bone, and slice the chicken into thin strips.

Soak the bread in 1 cup of the milk for 5 minutes. With your hands mash the bread and milk together to make a thick paste.

Heat the oil in a heavy skillet. Cook the remaining onions with the garlic for 5 minutes without browning. Meanwhile combine the dried chilies, *achiote,* and walnuts in a blender and grind fine. Add the bread paste and remaining cup of milk. Pour into the skillet and simmer, stirring, until the sauce thickens. Add the chicken and cheese and heat through.

3 hard-boiled eggs,
 quartered
12 black olives
2 fresh hot chilies or
 pimientos, cut in thin
 strips (pages 13–16)

Serve the mixture in a large, deep dish with the eggs, olives, and fresh chilies arranged in a spokelike pattern on top.

 SERVES 4 TO 6

ᴧᴧᴧᴧ CHICKEN SATÉ ᴧᴧᴧᴧ

Serve *satés* made from different meats as a main course and accompany them with small bowls of rice, vegetables, chutneys (see pages 261–263), *sambals* (see pages 264, 265, and 266), and slices of orange.

Peanut *Saté* Sauce (see page 248), Chili, Onion, and Tomato *Sambal* (see page 264), and Indonesian Cucumber Relish (see page 266) are all good accompaniments to this *saté*.

2 whole chicken breasts
3 tablespoons *ketjap*
 manis (page 9) or soy
 sauce
2 tablespoons lime juice
1 clove garlic, minced
2 tablespoons vegetable
 or peanut oil

Skin and bone the chicken breasts and cut them into ¾-inch squares. Marinate them in the *ketjap*, lime juice, and garlic for a few hours.

Thread the chicken pieces on skewers, brush with oil, and grill over hot coals or under a broiler.

 SERVES 4

⋀⋁⋀⋁ TURKEY MOLE POBLANO ⋀⋁⋀⋁

TURKEY PUEBLA-STYLE

In Mexico, this dish is made on special occasions. Chicken can also be used. Serve it with *Guacamole* (see page 67), tortillas, and rice. Lard is normally used, but peanut oil is healthier and lighter.

For a Shortcut *Mole* Sauce, see pages 246–247.

1 8- to 9-pound turkey, jointed and cut into pieces

Water to cover

4 tablespoons peanut oil

6 *ancho* chilies (page 13)

4 *pasilla* chilies (page 14)

6 *mulato* chilies (page 14)

2 slices white homemade-type bread

¼ pound shelled almonds

¼ pound shelled peanuts

2 medium onions, chopped

3 tomatoes, peeled and chopped (page 21)

3 cloves garlic, chopped

½ teaspoon ground cinnamon

½ teaspoon ground cloves

½ teaspoon anise

½ teaspoon ground coriander

1 teaspoon sugar

Simmer the turkey pieces in water to cover for about an hour. Drain, reserving liquid, and pat dry. Heat the peanut oil in a heavy skillet and brown the turkey. Remove and drain, reserving the oil in the pan.

Meanwhile prepare the chilies according to pages 15–16. Pour 2 cups of the turkey broth over them and soak them for 30 minutes.

In an electric blender grind the chilies, bread, almonds, peanuts, onions, tomatoes, and garlic to a coarse purée. Add the cinnamon, cloves, anise, coriander, and sugar. In the oil remaining in the skillet fry the mixture for 5 minutes, stirring constantly. Add 2 cups of turkey broth, chocolate, salt, and pepper. Bring to a boil.

Arrange the turkey pieces in an ovenproof dish. Pour the sauce over,

**1 1-ounce square
unsweetened chocolate**
**Coarse salt and freshly
ground black pepper**
**3 tablespoons sesame
seeds**

cover, and bake at 350 degrees for about 45 minutes. Sprinkle with sesame seeds and serve.

 **SERVES 8 TO 10**

MEAT

Most of the dishes in this chapter are excellent for entertaining because they improve if they are left overnight to develop their flavors. People with little time to cook after work can make them over a weekend or the night before.

It is more economical to buy large cuts of meat and cut them up yourself into the portions you need for stewing, etc. Buying meat from a butcher instead of at a supermarket may be more expensive, but in the long run you may well save money because he can suggest the correct cuts for the dishes you are making. Marinated meat can be kept for several days in the refrigerator and its flavor will be vastly improved. Freezing robs meat of taste and texture.

∿∿ BEEF ∿∿

The best beef is marbled with fat, has a deep red color, and is surrounded by a creamy layer of fat. If the meat is dark, dry, and the fat is yellow, it is old and stale. If packaged meat looks shiny and damp, it may have been frozen and thawed.

∿∿ LAMB ∿∿

Lamb absorbs flavor very well and is delicious with aromatic spices such as cumin, coriander, sesame seeds, paprika, and chili peppers. It becomes very tender when marinated. Good lamb has pale red flesh, white fat, and slightly translucent bones.

∿∿ PORK ∿∿

Pork responds quite well to marinades and is very good with chilies and hot spicy sauces. It has plenty of fat. It should be firm and pale pink and have no smell.

ᗯᐯᐯ VEAL ᗯᐯᐯ

Veal should be very pale pink with firm, satiny fat. Do not buy dark veal—it has not been fed solely on milk. Veal has a delicate flavor that it is a waste to cook such expensive meat in fiery sauces. The veal recipes in this chapter are therefore spicy but not overpowering.

ᗯᐯᐯ SPICED BEEF SATÉ ᗯᐯᐯ

2 pounds beef steak (any cut)

1 tablespoon coriander seed

2 fresh chilies, coarsely chopped (pages 13–16)

1 teaspoon turmeric

1 tablespoon fresh ginger, coarsely chopped

2 cloves garlic, peeled

1 medium onion, coarsely chopped

4 macadamia nuts

Melted *ghee* (page 38) or peanut oil

1 cup Coconut Milk (pages 36–37)

1 tablespoon brown sugar

2 tablespoons grated lemon peel

Coarse salt and freshly ground pepper

Cut the beef into 1-inch cubes. In an electric blender combine the coriander, chilies, turmeric, ginger, garlic, onion, and macadamia nuts. Add *ghee* or oil to keep the blades turning.

Heat a tablespoon of *ghee* or oil in a heavy skillet. Add the mixture and fry until thick. Pour in coconut milk, sugar, lemon peel; season with salt and pepper; and bring to a boil. Remove from heat.

Thread the beef cubes on small skewers (preferably wooden Oriental skewers) and grill under broiler or over hot coals, brushing generously with the sauce. Cook for 2 to 3 minutes, turning once. Serve the remainder of the sauce separately. Serve with rice.

☙ **SERVES 4 TO 6**

∿∿ KEFTA ∿∿

MOROCCAN MEATBALLS

These meatballs are made with ground spiced lamb or beef and are put on skewers and grilled over charcoal. You can vary the flavors. *Ras el Hanout* (see page 32) is often used. When you have spiced the meat, leave it for an hour or so, so that the flavor has time to develop.

The meat must contain at least 10 percent fat. You can grind your own at home in a meat grinder.

1½ pounds ground beef or lamb (or mixture)
1 small onion, grated
1 teaspoon ground cumin seed
2 teaspoons paprika
¼ cup chopped parsley or fresh coriander
½ teaspoon *Ras el Hanout* (page 32) (optional)
2 sprigs fresh mint, chopped
¼ teaspoon ground cinnamon
Coarse salt and freshly ground pepper

Combine all the ingredients in a mixing bowl. With wet hands, form mixture into 24 oblong-shaped patties and wrap them around skewers. Grill rapidly over high heat.

 SERVES 6

〜〜 STIR-FRIED BEEF, SZECHUAN-STYLE 〜〜

The cheaper cuts of steak are excellent here because this method of cooking prevents the meat from becoming tough.

1 pound butt steak
3 tablespoons dry sherry
3 tablespoons soy sauce
3 tablespoons sesame oil
2 cloves garlic, minced
2 tablespoons minced
  fresh ginger
3 scallions, chopped
  (including green part)
½ teaspoon ground
  Szechuan pepper
Coarse salt

Slice the steak against the grain into thin strips. Combine the sherry, soy sauce, 2 tablespoons of the sesame oil, garlic, and ginger and marinate the meat in this mixture for at least an hour (overnight if possible). Heat the remaining tablespoon of oil in a wok or skillet. Stir-fry the beef, including the marinade juice, for 2 to 3 minutes with the scallions. Do not overcook the meat or it will toughen. Season with salt and Szechuan pepper. Serve with boiled rice.

 **SERVES 2 TO 4**

〰 PICADILLO 〰

CUBAN-STYLE HASH

Serve with fried eggs, Fried Ripe Plantains (see page 191), boiled rice, or Mexican Beans (see page 206), as you choose.

2 pounds chopped lean beef

4 tablespoons *Achiote* Oil (page 34)

2 medium onions, finely chopped

4 green bell peppers, chopped

2 fresh chilies, chopped (pages 13–16)

2 cloves garlic, finely chopped

Coarse salt and freshly ground pepper

6 tomatoes, peeled and chopped (page 21)

2 cloves

2 apples, peeled and chopped

½ cup raisins

6 pimiento-stuffed olives, halved

¼ teaspoon ground cinnamon

2 tablespoons red wine vinegar

¼ cup slivered almonds

Brown the meat in the oil. Add the onions, peppers, chilies, garlic, salt, and pepper and cook for about 3 minutes, taking care to prevent burning. Add remaining ingredients except almonds and simmer about 25 minutes. Meanwhile fry the almonds in a little oil. Sprinkle over the meat. Serve immediately.

❧ SERVES 4 TO 6

MOROCCAN BEEF TAJINE
〜〜 **WITH CAULIFLOWER** 〜〜

3 pounds stewing beef (or
   lamb) cut into 1-inch
   cubes
¼ teaspoon turmeric
Coarse salt and freshly
   ground pepper
¼ cup peanut oil
1 medium onion, chopped
1 teaspoon ground ginger
Pinch pulverized saffron
1 tablespoon paprika
1 teaspoon ground cumin
¼ teaspoon cayenne
   pepper
2½ pounds cauliflower
Juice of 1 lemon
4 tablespoons chopped
   fresh coriander

Put the beef in a heavy casserole with
the turmeric, salt, pepper, and oil.
Brown, turn heat down, cover tightly,
and simmer for 15 minutes. Add onion and remaining spices, moisten
with a little water, and simmer 1½
hours, adding more water if necessary.

Steam the cauliflower, broken into
flowerets, until tender, set aside.

When meat is done, transfer to an
ovenproof dish with its sauce. Arrange the cauliflower over the top,
cover, and bake for 15 minutes in a
hot oven. Squeeze on the lemon juice,
sprinkle with coriander, and serve.

 **SERVES 6 TO 8**

ᗃᗃᗃ **ROPA VIEJA** ᗃᗃᗃ

CUBAN FLANK STEAK

Serve with Fried Ripe Plantains (see page 191) or Moors and Christians (Cuban Black Beans and Rice) (see page 216).

2 pounds flank steak
2 medium onions, chopped
1 carrot, sliced
1 turnip, peeled and cubed
1 bay leaf
Water to cover
3 tablespoons *Achiote* Oil
(page 34)
2 cloves garlic, minced
1 hot fresh chili pepper,
chopped (pages 13–16)
1 green bell pepper,
chopped
6 tomatoes, peeled and
chopped (page 21)
⅛ teaspoon ground
cinnamon
⅛ teaspoon ground cloves
Coarse salt and freshly
ground pepper
1 tablespoon capers
2 canned pimientos,
drained and finely
chopped

Put the steak in a heavy casserole with 1 onion, the carrot, turnip and bay leaf and pour in enough water to cover. Simmer for 1½ hours. When cool, shred it into pieces ¼ inch wide and 2 inches long. Set·meat and liquid aside.

Pour the oil into the casserole and fry the remaining onion, the garlic, chili pepper, and bell pepper. Watch carefully to prevent burning. Add the tomatoes and remaining spices. Season with salt and pepper. Cook until sauce is thick. Return meat to casserole with 2 cups of its cooking liquid. Simmer for 5 minutes. Add the capers. Garnish with pimiento and serve.

❦ **SERVES 4 TO 6**

ᴡᴡ **BEEF GOULASH** ᴡᴡ

Serve this Hungarian stew with noodles. Use Hungarian paprika.

3 tablespoons vegetable oil, lard, or bacon fat

4 medium onions, finely chopped

2 cloves garlic, finely chopped

2 tablespoons paprika

3 pounds stewing beef, cut in 1½-inch cubes

1 cup dry red wine

1 cup beef stock

Coarse salt and freshly ground pepper

1 teaspoon marjoram

Herb bouquet (parsley, thyme, celery leaves, and bay leaf tied in cheesecloth)

2 tablespoons flour

Heat the oil or fat in a heavy casserole that will go both on top of and inside of the stove. Fry the onions until golden with the garlic. Remove from heat, stir in the paprika and add the beef. Pour in the wine, stock, salt, pepper, and herbs. Cook in a preheated 350-degree oven for 1 hour. Skim off 2 tablespoons of fat and mix with the flour. Add the mixture to the stew and return to the oven for a further 30 to 40 minutes, or until beef is very tender. Remove herb bouquet before serving.

 **SERVES 4 TO 6**

∿∿ STEAK AU POIVRE ∿∿

This famous French dish consists of steaks cooked briskly with the coarse crushed peppercorns pressed into either side. To crush the peppercorns either use a pestle and mortar (a pepper mill will grind them too fine) or put them in a cloth and smash them with the back of a heavy frying pan or with a hammer.

Serve the steaks with baked potatoes.

1½ to 2 pounds boneless steaks (sirloin or filet mignon)

⅓ cup black peppercorns

1 tablespoon unsalted butter

1 tablespoon vegetable or peanut oil

¼ cup brandy

½ cup heavy cream

Coarse salt

Trim the fat from the steaks and crush the peppercorns. With the heel of your hand press the peppercorns firmly into the meat on both sides of the steaks. Heat the butter and oil in a heavy frying pan and cook the steaks over high heat. Remove to a warm plate. Remove from heat, add the brandy, then bring to a boil (taking care that the brandy does not flare up) and cook for 2 minutes (enough to boil off the alcohol), scraping up the cooking juices. Add the cream, heat through, season with salt, and pour over the steaks.

 SERVES 4

ᴡᴡᴡ SZÉKELY GULYÁS ᴡᴡᴡ

PORK AND SAUERKRAUT GOULASH

A famous goulash from Transylvania. The trick to making this famous goulash from Transylvania is not to dry out the sauerkraut. I suggest using a trivet under the casserole. Mashed potatoes and a bowl of sour cream are traditional accompaniments.

2 tablespoons vegetable oil, lard, or bacon fat
2 medium onions, chopped
1 clove garlic, chopped
1½ tablespoons Hungarian paprika
Coarse salt and freshly ground pepper
2 cups chicken or meat stock
2 pounds boneless pork, cut in 1-inch cubes
1 pound sauerkraut, washed and drained
1 tablespoon caraway seeds
2 tablespoons tomato purée
1 cup dry white wine
½ cup sour cream
½ cup heavy cream
1 tablespoon flour

Heat the oil or fat in a casserole and sauté the onions with the garlic until golden. Remove from heat, stir in the paprika. Season with salt and pepper and add about ½ cup of the stock, stir, and then add the pork. Arrange the sauerkraut in a layer over the pork, sprinkle with caraway seeds. Mix the tomato purée with the wine and remaining stock. Add, bring to a boil, turn down heat, and simmer 1 hour over very low heat, covered. Meanwhile, mix the sour cream and heavy cream with the flour until smooth. Add to the casserole when the meat is done, bring to a boil, and cook for a few minutes. Remove from heat and serve.

 **SERVES 4 TO 6**

∿∿ TRINIDAD PEPPER POT ∿∿

The equivalent of our Sunday roast, this spicy stew is served with boiled potatoes or yams and often lasts families for a week, bits and pieces being added daily to keep the stew going.

1 3- to 4-pound stewing chicken, cut up
1 pig's foot, split
3 pounds boneless pork or beef
Water to cover
Coarse salt and freshly ground pepper
2 medium onions, coarsely sliced
2 tablespoons dark brown sugar
2 fresh chilies, chopped
3-inch cinnamon stick
4 cloves
Dash thyme
1 tablespoon vinegar
1 tablespoon Worcestershire sauce

Simmer the chicken, pig's foot, and pork in water to cover for 1½ hours, skimming off any foam that may rise to the top. Add the remaining ingredients and cook for a further 30 minutes. Correct seasoning and serve.

 SERVES 8

SPICED BUTTERFLIED
∿∿ LEG OF LAMB ∿∿

Serve with rice and Turkish Cucumbers in Yogurt (see page 230).

1 5- to 6-pound leg of
  lamb, boned and
  butterflied so it lies flat
2 cloves garlic, peeled
2 tablespoons chopped
  fresh ginger
1 tablespoon paprika
2 teaspoon ground cumin
1 teaspoon ground
  coriander
2 tablespoons fresh mint
  leaves, chopped
½ cup plain yogurt
¼ cup peanut oil
Coarse salt to taste

Place the lamb in a large, shallow, noncorrosive dish. Combine the rest of the ingredients and spread them over the meat. Marinate overnight, turning the lamb from time to time. Bring the lamb to room temperature before it is cooked.

Preheat broiler or coals. Remove meat from marinade, reserving the marinade, and scrape off any excess. Put the meat on an oiled rack and broil for about 7 to 8 minutes on each side, depending on how rare or well done you like it. As it cooks, baste with the marinade. Let it rest for 5 minutes before carving.

 **YIELD: 8 TO 10 SERVINGS**

ᴡᴡᴡ SPICED LAMB SATÉ ᴡᴡᴡ

Serve with Indonesian Hot Pepper Relish (see page 267) or *Sambal Ketjap* (see page 265).

2 pounds boned lamb, cut in cubes
2 cloves garlic, minced
2 hot fresh chilies, minced (pages 13–16)
1 teaspoon ground cumin
½ teaspoon ground allspice
½ teaspoon ground ginger
1 cup red wine vinegar
4 tablespoons brown sugar
4 tablespoons peanut oil
Coarse salt and freshly ground pepper

Marinate the lamb in the garlic, chilies, and spices at room temperature for an hour. Mix the remaining ingredients and pour onto the lamb. Leave for a couple of hours at room temperature or refrigerate overnight.

Remove meat from marinade and set aside. Thread the meat on Oriental wooden skewers and grill over hot coals or under broiler until the meat is crisp and done according to your taste. Baste with the marinade. Serve with rice as a main course, accompanied by a sauce, or as an appetizer with sauce.

 YIELD: 8 SKEWERS

∿∿ LAMB SATÉ ∿∿

This can be served as a main course with rice or as an appetizer. Indonesian Hot Pepper Relish (see page 267) or *Sambal Ketjap* (see page 265) is good with it.

2 pounds boneless lamb, cut in cubes
¼ cup *ketjap manis* (page 9) or dark soy sauce
2 cloves garlic, minced
Juice of half a lemon
1 tablespoon minced fresh ginger

Marinate the lamb for a few hours at room temperature (or refrigerated overnight) in the remaining ingredients. Thread on small skewers (wooden Oriental ones are the best) and broil over charcoal or under a grill until crisp, depending on how well done you like them.

 **YIELD: 8 SKEWERS**

LAMB SATÉ
∿∿ IN MACADAMIA NUT SAUCE ∿∿

LAMB
2 pounds boneless lamb, cubed
2 cloves garlic, minced
2 tablespoons dark soy sauce
Coarse salt and freshly ground pepper

SAUCE
1 medium onion, finely chopped

To prepare the lamb, marinate it for an hour at room temperature (or refrigerate overnight) in the garlic, soy sauce, salt, and pepper.

To prepare the sauce, combine the remaining ingredients in a small saucepan with a little water and simmer for 20 minutes, or until onion is soft.

6 macadamia nuts, ground

1 fresh *serrano* pepper, minced (page 15)

Juice of half a lime or lemon

½ cup *ketjap manis* (page 9) or dark soy sauce

2 tablespoons brown sugar (omit if using *ketjap manis*)

Thread the lamb on small skewers (wooden Oriental ones are the best) and grill over hot coals or under a broiler until done according to your taste. Baste with the marinade. Serve the sauce separately.

🌰 **YIELD: 8 SKEWERS**

〜〜 PORK SATÉ 〜〜

Peanut *Saté* Sauce (see page 248), *Sambal Ketjap* (see page 265), and Indonesian Cucumber Relish (see page 267) are the sauces and relishes that go best with this *saté*. Serve with white rice and a vegetable.

2 pound boneless pork butt

1 tablespoon ground coriander

1 medium onion, chopped

1 clove garlic, chopped

1 hot green chili, chopped (pages 14–16)

1-inch piece of fresh ginger, grated

3 tablespoons lime or lemon juice

Coarse salt to taste

2 tablespoons peanut or vegetable oil

Cut the pork into ¾-inch cubes. Combine the remaining ingredients (except the oil) in a blender and blend, adding a little water to make the mixture into a paste. Coat the pork cubes with the mixture and allow to marinate for several hours.

Thread the pork on skewers, brush with oil, and cook over hot coals or under a broiler.

🌰 **YIELD: 8 SKEWERS**

∿∿ PORK CHOPS CHARCUTIÈRE ∿∿

Serve these with browned potatoes.

4 thick pork chops
Flour
Coarse salt and freshly
**   ground pepper**
4 tablespoons butter
4 tomatoes, peeled and
**   chopped (page 21)**
½ cup water
1 tablespoon chopped
**   shallots**
¼ cup white wine
1 teaspoon vinegar
2 teaspoons prepared
**   mustard**
2 tablespoons chopped
**   pickles**
1 tablespoon chopped
**   parsley**

Trim the pork chops, dredge them with seasoned flour, and fry them in 2 tablespoons of the butter for about 12 to 15 minutes on each side. Meanwhile, in a separate pan, cook the tomatoes in 1 tablespoon of the butter with the water until you have a thick purée. Set aside.

When the chops are cooked, remove to a dish and keep warm. Melt the remaining butter in the frying pan and fry the shallots without browning. Add the white wine, vinegar, tomato purée, mustard, and pickles, and bring to a boil. Correct the seasoning, pour the mixture over the chops, sprinkle with parsley, and serve.

 SERVES 4

〰〰 **MANCHA MANTELES DE CERDO** 〰〰

PORK TABLECLOTH STAINER

**2 pounds boneless pork,
   cubed**
1 bay leaf
½ teaspoon oregano
½ teaspoon thyme
3 *mulato* chilies (page 14)
2 *ancho* chilies (page 13)
1 *pasilla* chili (page 14)
**4 tomatoes, peeled (page
   21)**
**1 medium onion, coarsely
   chopped**
4 sprigs fresh coriander
2 garlic cloves, minced
**¼ teaspoon powdered
   cloves**
**¼ teaspoon ground
   cinnamon**
½ teaspoon ground cumin
3 tablespoons peanut oil
**2 sweet potatoes, cooked
   and cubed**
2 tart apples, sliced
2 large bananas, sliced
1 cup green peas
**Coarse salt and freshly
   ground pepper**

Simmer the pork in a heavy casserole with the bay leaf, oregano, and thyme for 1½ hours. Meanwhile prepare the chilies according to instructions on pages 15–16.

Combine the chilies, tomatoes, onion, coriander, garlic, cloves, cinnamon, and cumin in a blender. Blend until smooth. Heat the peanut oil in a large pan and add the mixture. Cook for 5 minutes, then stir in 1½ cups of the pork stock. Add the pork, remaining fruits and vegetables, and salt and pepper to taste and simmer for 30 minutes.

🌶 SERVES 4

∿∿ TEXAS CHILI CON CARNE ∿∿

Serve this with pinto beans and rice.

6 *pequín* chilies (page 14)
6 *ancho* chilies (page 13)
2 pounds stewing beef, cut
in ½-inch cubes
1 tablespoon olive oil
2 bay leaves
1 tablespoon cumin seed
2 cloves garlic, peeled
2 teaspoons oregano
2 tablespoons paprika
1 teaspoon sugar
Coarse salt and freshly
ground pepper

Tear the chilies in strips and pour 2 cups of boiling water over them. Let soak for 30 minutes. Drain, reserving the liquid, and set aside. Heat the oil in a heavy skillet and brown the beef cubes. Add the chili-soaking liquid and bring to a boil. Add the bay leaves, turn down the heat, and let simmer for an hour. Add more water as needed. Meanwhile, purée the remaining ingredients, including the chilies, with a little water if needed, in an electric blender. Add the purée to the meat and let simmer for 30 minutes more.

 SERVES 4

AMERICAN INDIAN
ᗢᗢᗢ BARBECUED PORK ROAST ᗢᗢᗢ

The resultant sauce from this roast is much like Mexican *mole poblano* sauce; the chocolate and the chilies give it a rich dark color. Rice, Fried Ripe Plantains (see page 191), and a green vegetable would be good with it. So would Mexican Beans (see page 206).

½ cup peanut or
   vegetable oil

3 medium onions, chopped

3 cloves garlic, chopped

1 teaspoon crushed
   coriander seed

6 juniper berries, crushed

1 bay leaf

2 pounds tomatoes,
   peeled

¾ cup tarragon vinegar

1 cup water

1 teaspoon crushed red
   chili pepper

1 tablespoon chili powder

Coarse salt and freshly
   ground pepper

5½-pound pork roast

In a saucepan heat the oil and sauté the onions with the garlic until soft. Add the remaining ingredients (except pork) and simmer gently for 45 minutes, covered.

Arrange the trimmed roast in a roasting pan and bake in a preheated 350-degree oven for about 3½ hours, basting with the sauce.

🌶 SERVES 6

∿∿ TWICE-COOKED SZECHUAN PORK ∿∿

1 pound boneless pork
Water to cover
3 tablespoons peanut,
    vegetable, or sesame oil
2 cloves garlic, minced
2 tablespoons chopped
    fresh ginger
1 leek, chopped
½ cup bamboo shoots
1 green bell pepper,
    chopped
½ teaspoon crushed
    Szechuan pepper
1 teaspoon sugar
4 tablespoons *hoisin*
    sauce

Simmer the pork (in one piece) in water to cover for 20 minutes. Remove, drain (reserving the liquid), and cut into pieces 1-inch square and ¼-inch thick. Heat the oil in a wok or skillet and stir-fry the pork cubes. Add the garlic, ginger, vegetables, and peppers. Stir-fry for 2 to 3 minutes. Add 2 tablespoons of the pork cooking liquid and remaining ingredients. Stir and cook for another minute. Remove and serve with plain white rice.

 SERVES 2 TO 4

CHINESE PORK AND SHRIMP
∿∿ WITH PEPPERS ∿∿

1 pound boneless pork,
    diced
3 tablespoons soy sauce
2 tablespoons dry sherry
1 clove garlic, minced
4 tablespoons peanut or
    vegetable oil
3 scallions, chopped
    (including green part)
3 bell peppers (red and
    green), chopped

Marinate the pork in the soy sauce, sherry, and garlic for a couple of hours at room temperature (or refrigerate overnight).

Drain the meat, reserving the marinade. Heat the oil in a skillet and stir-fry the meat for 3 minutes. Add the scallions, peppers, chilies, and zucchini and stir-fry for 3 more minutes. Add the shrimp, stir-fry for 1

2 hot fresh chilies, diced
(pages 13–16)
2 small zucchini, cut in thin
strips
4 large shrimp, peeled
and cut in ¾-inch pieces
1 tablespoon sesame oil
Coarse salt and freshly
ground black pepper

minute, stir in the marinade and sesame oil and season with salt and pepper. Serve with rice.

❧ SERVES 3 TO 4

∿∿ HUNGARIAN VEAL PAPRIKASH ∿∿

2 pounds stewing veal
1 tablespoon peanut or
vegetable oil
2 tablespoons butter
3 small onions, sliced
1 clove garlic, minced
1 green pepper, seeded
and chopped
1 tablespoon flour
2 tablespoons Hungarian
paprika (or more to
taste)
2 cups tomatoes, peeled,
seeded, and chopped
(page 21)
2 cups water
½ cup sour cream
Coarse salt and freshly
ground pepper to taste

Pat the veal dry and cut into 1-inch cubes. Set aside. Put the oil and butter in a large, heavy casserole and soften the onions with the garlic and pepper. Add the veal and sprinkle with the flour and paprika. Cook, turning frequently, for 3 to 4 minutes. When the drippings begin to dry up add a little of the water and scrape them up.

Add the remaining water and the tomatoes and cook, stirring frequently, for about 30 to 40 minutes, or until the veal is tender. Just before serving, stir in the sour cream and correct the seasoning.

❧ SERVES 4

NOTE: This is good with noodles.

ᴠᴠᴠ **MUSTARD KIDNEYS** ᴠᴠᴠ

2 veal kidneys

2 shallots, minced

2 tablespoons unsalted butter

¼ to ½ cup dry red wine or cognac

2 tablespoons Dijon mustard

Coarse salt and freshly ground pepper to taste

Trim the fat from the kidneys and slice them in pieces about ¾-inch thick. Soften the shallots in the butter. Add the kidneys and brown lightly for 1 to 2 minutes. Add the wine and mustard and stir thoroughly. Season with salt and pepper and cook over medium heat until the kidneys are done to your taste (do not overcook or they will be tough and dry—medium rare is the best and this should not take more than 2 to 3 minutes).

🍃 **SERVES 2**

NOTE: Serve with rice or mashed potatoes.

ᐁᐁᐁ BRITISH DEVILED KIDNEYS ᐁᐁᐁ

Serve these on toast for a light supper dish. Rice, a green vegetable, and grilled tomatoes would be typical British accompaniments.

4 veal or 8 lamb kidneys
2 tablespoons mango chutney
1 tablespoon Dijon mustard
1½ tablespoons dry mustard
Cayenne pepper to taste
Oil
Coarse salt and freshly ground pepper

Remove the inside filament from the kidneys carefully, using a pointed knife or a pair of nail scissors. Wipe the kidneys with paper towels. In a bowl big enough to hold the meat, combine the chutney, mustards, and cayenne, using the cayenne according to how spicy you would like the kidneys to be. Let stand for a couple of hours at room temperature.

Put the kidneys in a broiling pan, preferably on a rack, brush with a little oil, and grill quickly under high heat, about 3 minutes on each side. Do not overcook or they will become tough. Scrape up the juices, season with salt and pepper, and pour over the kidneys.

 SERVES 4

GRILLED MERGUEZ WITH COUSCOUS
〜〜〜 AND STEAMED VEGETABLES 〜〜〜

In Morocco they make a delicious spicy sausage out of lamb called *merguez*. It is available at some of the more enterprising butchers, depending on where you live. *Chorizo,* the peppery Latin sausage, may be used in its place. This is a simple dish, very quick to prepare. It's not an authentic *couscous,* because I use the instant kind here, served with steamed vegetables. But I make no apologies for this dish: It's perfect when you feel like rustling up something that's easy to prepare, but a little out of the ordinary. If you like, serve it with *Harissa* Sauce (see page 265).

4 carrots, sliced

4 medium potatoes, sliced

3 medium zucchini, sliced

1½ pounds *merguez* sausages

1 1-pound package instant *couscous*

Chicken broth in amount specified on *couscous* package

1 pinch pulverized saffron

1 tablespoon butter

3 tablespoons fresh coriander, chopped

Preheat broiler. Steam the vegetables until they are cooked. Meanwhile, broil the sausages. Make the *couscous* according to the directions on the package (it will take about 5 minutes), using chicken broth instead of water and adding the saffron to it. Fluff up the *couscous* with a fork, adding the butter, and empty out onto a serving dish. Top with the vegetables. Arrange the sausages around and sprinkle with coriander.

 SERVES 4

CURRY

〰〰

To many Westerners curry still means a fiery Indian sauce, deep yellow in color and thickened with flour, used indiscriminately with fish, meat, or chicken, accompanied by Major Grey's chutney and a mound of sticky rice. But the recent popularity of Indian restaurants and Indian specialty shops proves that many people are discovering the extraordinary variety of dishes that make up Indian and Pakistani cuisine. India and Pakistan cover a huge area; the food is radically different in each region. The United States must be the only country in the world where you can drive 500 miles and still find the same food at the end of your journey.

There are hundreds of curries, as many as there are stews in Western cooking. Each is made with different ingredients, and is distinct in flavor and hotness. Some are very delicate, some hot, and all obtain their flavors from ingenious use of spices. The rich colors; the appetizing aroma; the long slow cooking that produces a pungent, hot, or delicate sauce; and the simple techniques—all combine to tempt people to try curries for themselves. They are marvelous for entertaining because they can be made the night before and improve the next day. Remember, though, that hot curries get even hotter as the flavors develop. Cold curries are also good and make excellent dishes for summer entertaining.

The word *curry* comes from the Indian word *kari,* which means sauce. In India, this sauce is made from a mixture of spices prepared by the cook. Indians do not use all-purpose commercial powders. These are often made from the cheapest ingredients and have a harsh taste and a flatness about them that makes all curries taste alike.

Aromatics are the heart of Indian cooking. A good curry must be made with fresh home-ground spices. These should be stored in a cool place in a sealed container and away from light. Chilies and mustard seeds produce the heat in a curry. Cornstarch and flour are almost never used as thickening agents; turmeric and onions do that job. The juices from the meat or vegetables, yogurt, or coconut milk also provide the sauce base and thickening agent. Tomatoes are not typical ingredients in an Indian curry; they tend sometimes to mask the other flavors and should be used with care. Depending on the browning of the meat and on the spices and aromatics used, curries can be dark red or brown, green, or light gold in color.

The basic "curry powder" is known as *masala,* and the proportions and balance of this *masala* are tremendously important. After trying a few combinations, most cooks settle on a mixture that suits their taste. And it's not so much which spices you use, but how you use them that makes a difference. Some spices are fried in *ghee* (clarified butter, see page 38) and added at the beginning; others are added toward the end. Cheap ingredients should never be used. You will waste your money because the results will be poor. Use fresh ingredients and experiment with *ghee,* or try using mustard oil or coconut oil. Meat cooked in mustard oil can be kept for weeks, according to Indian sources. All the spices used in curries are preservatives and have antiseptic value. For advice on grinding your own spices see the chapter on powders and pastes.

Madras curries are very hot and pungent; the sauce is quite thin. *Bengal* curries are cooked in mustard oil and served with rice. *Punjab* curries are eaten with lentils and flat, unleavened wholewheat bread. *Bombay* food is cosmopolitan and the curries are highly spiced, using a lot of red-hot chilies. *Korma* curries are made with meat or vegetables braised with water or stock, yogurt or cream. There are many different textures and tastes; the meat should be lean, and *ghee,* not oil, is used. *Kebab* curries are meat threaded on skewers and simmered in a spiced gravy. *Kofta* curries are meat or chicken balls cooked in a curry sauce, while *keema* curries are made with ground meat. *Vindaloo* is a sour curry of meat or seafood marinated in a well-spiced vinegar marinade for several hours before cooking.

Curry should be accompanied by rice that is white and dry, with each grain separate. Saffron Rice, Caribbean-Style (see page 212) may also be used. See pages 211–212 for further information on cooking rice. The accompaniments should be arranged attractively in little dishes. Lentils (*Dal*, see page 219) and Indian breads may accompany curries. Try local Indian shops for ideas. For a small gathering or family meal, a curry dinner could consist of a main dish, a vegetable, rice, chutney, and yogurt. For a large group, serve a meat curry, a fish curry, lentils, rice, two or three vegetable dishes, pickles, various chutneys, yogurt, and salad.

The essential thing is to get the right balance of food. Serve a dry dish with a moist one, a bland curry with a fiery one, a chilled dish and a hot one, a sweet dish and a sour one, a preserved chutney and a fresh one.

CONDIMENTS FOR CURRY

In addition to chutneys, pickles, and relishes, these condiments can be served with curry. Arrange them in little bowls on the table. If you are entertaining, keep extra condiments in the refrigerator in case you run out. Store them in plastic bags. If you don't need them at once, they will come in handy for other dishes later.

Sliced bananas with lemon juice squeezed on them	Yogurt (pages 37–38)
	Grated coconut
Chopped apples with lemon juice squeezed on them	Chopped parsley
	Chopped chives
Chopped peanuts	Chopped scallions
Chopped tomatoes	Raisins
Chopped onion	Chopped hard-boiled eggs
Sliced cucumbers	

〰️ WHOLE EGG CURRY 〰️

This is an attractive dish for a party. Serve it with rice, chutney, and condiments. It improves if made the day before.

12 hard-boiled eggs
¼ pound slivered almonds
1 tablespoon ground saffron
¼ tablespoon turmeric
4 tablespoons lime juice
1 tablespoon dried ground chili peppers (pages 13–16)
1 teaspoon garlic, minced
1 bay leaf, ground
2 cups plain yogurt
½ cup heavy cream
Coarse salt and freshly ground pepper
½ cup chicken stock (more or less as necessary)
1 tablespoon roasted sesame seeds
Chopped chives to garnish

Peel the eggs and stick them all over with almond slivers. Make gashes down to the yolk, but not right through. Combine the saffron, turmeric, lime juice, chili peppers, garlic, and bay leaf. Coat the eggs with this mixture.

In a large saucepan heat the yogurt and the cream and add the eggs. Season with salt and pepper, bring to a boil, and simmer over medium heat, adding stock if necessary, until sauce is thick. Sprinkle with sesame seeds and chives, and serve.

 **SERVES 6 TO 8**

〰〰 VEGETABLE CURRY 〰〰

This can be served on its own or with a meat or egg curry.

4 tablespoons peanut or vegetable oil
4 medium onions, sliced
4 cloves garlic, chopped
½ tablespoon chili powder
2 tablespoons Mild Curry Powder (page 26)
½ tablespoon turmeric
½ tablespoon coriander seed
1 bay leaf
6 cloves
½ teaspoon ground cinnamon
1 teaspoon sugar
6 tomatoes, chopped
6 carrots, chopped
4 small turnips, diced (or 2 large ones)
2 pounds potatoes, diced
6 stalks celery with leaves, chopped
2 cups lentils
Water or stock to cover
¾ pound green beans, cut in 1½-inch pieces
1 10-ounce can chick-peas
Coarse salt and freshly ground black pepper

Heat the oil in a large pot. Soften the onions with the garlic and add the chili powder, curry powder, turmeric, coriander seeds, and bay leaf. Cook, stirring, for 3 minutes. Add the cloves, cinnamon, sugar, and tomatoes. Cook for another 2 minutes. Add the remaining ingredients except the green beans and chick-peas. Simmer gently for about an hour, or until the potatoes, lentils, and carrots are cooked. Put in more water if curry seems too dry. Add the beans and cook for 10 minutes. Add peas, heat through, season with salt and pepper, and serve.

🌿 SERVES 8 TO 10

〰〰 POTATO CURRY 〰〰

This is very good with new potatoes. Serve as a vegetable or with curry. If you are cooking for a large number of people, this curry makes a great side dish.

1 medium onion, chopped
1 tablespoon *ghee* (page 38) or butter
2 tablespoons chopped fresh coriander or parsley
1 teaspoon turmeric
½ teaspoon chili powder
Coarse salt
1 pound potatoes, cut small
1 teaspoon *Garam Masala* (page 27)
Juice of half a lemon

Fry the onion in the *ghee* until golden. Add the coriander, turmeric, chili powder, and salt, and fry for a few minutes. Add the potatoes and a little water. Cook over low heat for about 30 minutes. For the last 10 minutes of cooking time add the *masala* and lemon juice.

 SERVES 4

〰〰 BANANA CURRY 〰〰

This is a side dish and goes well with large curry dinners. Use slightly underripe bananas.

1½ pounds bananas
Juice of half a lemon
1 tablespoon *ghee* (page 38) or butter
½ teaspoon turmeric
1 teaspoon caraway seeds

Slice the bananas and squeeze a little lemon juice on them to prevent them from turning brown. Heat the *ghee* and add the turmeric and caraway seeds. Fry for a couple of minutes, then add the bananas with the chili.

½ **teaspoon dried ground chilies (pages 13—16)**
¼ **cup yogurt**
½ **teaspoon** *Garam Masala* **(page 27)**
Coarse salt

Cook for about 5 minutes, then add remaining ingredients and cook for 10 minutes.

 SERVES 4

 SIMPLE CHICKEN CURRY

Serve with rice and condiments suggested on page 175.

1 3- to 4-pound frying chicken, cut up
2 tablespoons *ghee* **(page 38) or butter**
2 medium onions, chopped
2 cloves garlic, chopped
2 teaspoons *Garam Masala* **(page 27)**
Water or stock to cover
Coarse salt and freshly ground pepper

Dry the chicken pieces with paper towels. Heat the *ghee* in a heavy-bottomed casserole and fry the chicken until golden. Remove and set aside. Soften the onions and garlic in the *ghee*. Add the *masala* and cook, stirring, for 2 minutes, taking care to prevent burning. Add the stock or water, season with salt and pepper, and return the chicken to the casserole. Simmer gently until chicken is done, about 30 to 45 minutes.

 SERVES 4

∿∿ TRINIDAD SHRIMP CURRY ∿∿

Serve with boiled rice and Green Mango Chutney (see page 261).

2 pounds large shrimp

1½ teaspoons ground cumin

1½ teaspoons ground coriander

1½ teaspoons mustard seeds

1½ teaspoons peppercorns

1½ teaspoons turmeric

½ teaspoon crushed red hot pepper

1 bay leaf

4 tablespoons *ghee* (page 38) or 2 tablespoons peanut oil and 2 tablespoons butter

2 onions, finely chopped

2 cloves garlic, minced

1 tablespoon chopped fresh ginger

4 tomatoes, peeled and chopped (page 21)

Juice of 1 lime

Coarse salt and freshly ground pepper

Water as necessary

Shell the shrimp and devein them. Combine the spices in an electric grinder or pound together using a pestle and mortar. In a large, heavy skillet heat the *ghee*. Fry the onions with the garlic and ginger without browning. Add the ground spices and cook for 3 minutes, taking care not to burn the mixture. Add the tomatoes and lime juice, season with salt and pepper, and simmer gently for 30 minutes, adding water if the sauce becomes dry.

Add the shrimp and coat them with the sauce. Cook, covered, for 5 minutes. Be careful not to overcook them; they should be juicy and pink. Serve immediately.

 SERVES 4

ᴡᴡ BHUNA CHICKEN ᴡᴡ

This is a "dry" curry, meaning that it is cooked without stock or other liquid. Cook it over very low heat, preferably on a trivet. Serve it with rice.

1 3- to 3½-pound chicken, cut up and skinned
1 medium onion, chopped
2 cloves garlic, finely chopped
2 tablespoons *ghee* (page 38) or butter
1 teaspoon turmeric
2 teaspoons *Garam Masala* (page 27)
1 teaspoon chili powder
3 tomatoes, peeled and chopped (page 21)
1 tablespoon lemon juice
1 tablespoon grated coconut
Coarse salt
Fresh chopped coriander to garnish

Dry the chicken with paper towels. Fry the onion with the garlic in the *ghee* until golden. Add the remaining ingredients (except coriander), turning the chicken so that it is thoroughly coated with the spices. Cover tightly and cook over very low heat for about 1 hour. Sprinkle with coriander.

 SERVES 4

ᨠᨠᨠ THAI CHICKEN CURRY ᨠᨠᨠ

Use either red or green paste for this curry. Prepare the coconut milk in advance. Serve the curry with rice and a *sambal*.

3 cups Coconut Milk (pages 36–37)

2 tablespoons Thai Curry Paste (page 29)

4 chicken breasts, boned and cut into inch-long strips

2 tablespoons bottled fish sauce (page 9)

Coarse salt

Chopped fresh basil to garnish

2 chopped fresh red or green chilies

Bring 1 cup of the coconut milk to a boil. Add the paste and simmer for about 5 minutes. Add the chicken, the remaining coconut milk, and fish sauce and simmer for about 15 minutes, until the chicken is cooked and the sauce has reduced. Season with salt, sprinkle with basil and chilies.

 SERVES 4

∿∿ CHICKEN KORMA ∿∿

2 2½-pound chickens, cut
up

2 cups yogurt

3 cloves garlic, chopped

2 medium onions, chopped

1 teaspoon paprika

2 teaspoons fresh ginger,
finely chopped

Coarse salt and freshly
ground pepper to taste

4 tablespoons butter or
ghee (page 38)

3 teaspoons ground
coriander

½ teaspoon dried ground
chilies (pages 13–16)

2 teaspoons ground cumin

2 cardamom seeds

1 teaspoon poppy seeds

1 tablespoon turmeric

Water to cover

1 bay leaf

2 tablespoons chopped
fresh mint leaves
(optional)

Place the chicken in a bowl and marinate for a few hours in the yogurt, 1 clove garlic, half an onion, paprika, ginger, salt, and pepper

Melt the butter in a large heavy pan and fry the remaining onions and garlic until golden. Remove, and add the coriander, chili, cumin, cardamom, poppy seeds, and turmeric. Fry for a few minutes. Add the chicken pieces, sear, and then pour in enough water to cover and any remaining marinade. Return the onions and garlic, add the bay leaf and mint, and simmer for about 45 minutes, or until chicken is tender.

🌿 SERVES 6

〰 **KOFTA CURRY** 〰

Koftas are little meatballs and make a good, economical curry. Serve the curry with rice and a fresh chutney. You may also make the meatballs without the sauce and serve them on toothpicks as an hors d'oeuvre, using the chutney as a dip.

MEATBALLS

1 medium onion, finely chopped

2 cloves garlic, finely chopped

½ green bell pepper, finely chopped

1 tablespoon *ghee* (page 38) or butter

2 tablespoons fresh coriander or parsley, chopped

Coarse salt and freshly ground pepper

1½ pounds ground meat (beef, lamb, or pork)

1 tablespoon *Garam Masala* (page 27)

½ tablespoon chili powder

1 egg

Oil for deep frying

CURRY SAUCE

1 medium onion, chopped

1-inch piece of fresh ginger, chopped

To prepare the meatballs, soften the onion with the garlic and pepper in the *ghee*. Combine in a bowl with the remaining ingredients for meatballs (except the oil). Form into balls (golf-ball size) and fry in oil until brown.

To make the curry sauce, soften the onion with the ginger in the *ghee*. Add the spices, cook for a couple of minutes, then add the tomatoes and a little stock. Bring to a boil and when thickened slightly add the meatballs with more stock to cover if necessary. Heat through and serve.

 SERVES 4

1 tablespoon *ghee* (page
   38) or butter
1 teaspoon turmeric
½ teaspoon chili powder
½ teaspoon *Garam
   Masala* (page 27)
1½ pounds tomatoes,
   peeled and chopped
   (page 21)
Stock to cover

⌁⌁ KEEMA CURRY ⌁⌁

The curry will be much improved if you mince your own meat with a meat grinder. Serve this curry with *Chapattis* (see page 217) and rice.

1 tablespoon *ghee* (page
   38) or butter
1 medium onion, chopped
2 cloves garlic, chopped
2 tablespoons fresh
   coriander or parsley,
   chopped
1 pound ground beef
1 teaspoon turmeric
½ teaspoon chili powder
4 tomatoes, peeled and
   chopped
Coarse salt
1 tablespoon *Garam
   Masala* (page 27)
1 cup peas

Heat the *ghee* and fry the onion with the garlic until golden. Add the coriander, meat, turmeric, and chili powder. Bring to a boil, add tomatoes and salt and cook over very low heat (on a trivet if possible) for 30 minutes. Add the *garam masala* and the peas. Cook for another 15 to 20 minutes.

✿ SERVES 4

EAST AFRICAN BEEF
〰〰 **AND PLANTAIN CURRY** 〰〰

4 plantains

Boiling water

1½ pounds boneless beef,
cubed

3 tablespoons olive oil or
ghee (page 38)

2 medium onions, chopped

2 carrots, sliced

1 leek, chopped

3 cloves garlic, minced

¾ teaspoon turmeric

1 teaspoon dried ground
chilies (pages 13–16)

½ teaspoon ground cumin

½ teaspoon ground
coriander

½ teaspoon caraway
seeds

1 3-inch cinnamon stick

½ teaspoon ground
ginger

1½ tablespoons flour

1½ cups tomato purée

Coarse salt and freshly
ground pepper

½ cup red wine

Slice the plantains and simmer for 15 minutes in boiling water. Brown the beef in the oil, add the onions, carrots, leek, and garlic. Fry until golden, add the spices, cook for 2 minutes, then add the flour. Cook for 2 or 3 minutes, taking care to prevent burning. Add the tomato purée, salt, pepper, and wine, and bring to a boil. Simmer for 25 minutes. Add water if curry seems dry. Add the plantains and simmer for 25 minutes.

 SERVES 4

〰〰 BEEF VINDALOO 〰〰

A hot, spicy, sweet-sour curry, serve this with white rice and chutney. If possible leave the meat overnight in the paste and leave it again for another night once it has been cooked.

1½ pounds boneless beef

2 to 3 tablespoons Indian Vindaloo Paste (page 28)

3 tablespoons *ghee* (page 38)

Water

Coarse salt

Cut the beef into 1½-inch cubes and pat dry with paper towels. Put the meat in a large bowl and toss thoroughly to coat with the paste. Allow to marinate for at least 4 hours.

Melt the *ghee* in a heavy casserole. Fry the beef carefully to prevent burning it, and add enough water to make a gravy. Season with salt. Cover and cook over low heat for about 1½ hours or until the meat is tender.

 SERVES 4

〰〰 SIMPLE LAMB BIRYANI 〰〰

A popular Moslem dish, serve this with chutney.

2 pounds boneless lamb
1 teaspoon ground
   coriander
½ teaspoon ground cloves
½ teaspoon ground
   cardamom
¼ teaspoon dried ground
   chilies (pages 13—16)
½ teaspoon ground cumin
½ teaspoon ground
   cinnamon
Coarse salt and freshly
   ground pepper
1-inch piece of fresh
   ginger, chopped
3 cloves garlic, chopped
Juice of 1 lemon
2 cups yogurt
2 medium onions
2 tablespoons *ghee* (page
   38) or butter
3 cups Patna rice, cooked
   (page 211)

Cut the lamb into cubes and marinate for a few hours in a mixture of the spices, ginger, garlic, lemon juice, and yogurt. Fry the onions in the *ghee* until soft, add the lamb and a little water to make a gravy for the lamb to cook in. Cover, and cook over low heat until done (about 1½ hours).

In a heavy casserole layer alternately the rice and the lamb, finishing with the rice. Bake in a low oven, about 300 degrees, for half an hour.

 SERVES 4

VEGETABLES

n many countries where hot food is eaten, people are either vegetarian or eat very little meat. As a result, countless interesting recipes for vegetables cooked with hot spices have been developed. Some of the vegetable dishes in this chapter are good as side dishes in buffets. Two or three can be combined and served as a main course, accompanied perhaps by white rice and a couple of relishes or table sauces.

Vegetables should not be cooked in large amounts of boiling water. Unless they are cooked in the sauce in which they are to be served, they should be steamed. They should be bright in color, crisp, and fresh. Steaming preserves the vitamins and minerals that would dissolve in water.

FRIED RIPE PLANTAINS ᨆᨆ OR BANANAS ᨆᨆ

These are delicious with Mexican or Caribbean dishes. Use greenish bananas if you cannot get ripe plantains. Overripe bananas will not hold their shape.

Plantains or bananas
Lemon or lime juice
Peanut oil
Coarse salt

Peel and slice the bananas (lengthwise or in rounds, according to your preference—and the size of the bananas) and squeeze lemon juice over them. Heat enough oil to cover the bottom of a heavy skillet and fry until golden brown. Season with coarse salt and serve immediately.

 **YIELD: 1 BANANA PER PERSON**

MEXICAN STRING BEANS
∿∿ WITH CHILIES ∿∿

An excellent way to cook the rather large string beans that are available fresh in the market. These beans go very well with lamb or pork chops; fried, grilled, or roast chicken; or grilled fish.

Use fresh green or red chilies if available; if not, use canned chilies.

1 tablespoon peanut, vegetable, or olive oil

1 medium onion, chopped

1 clove garlic, chopped (optional)

2 chilies, chopped (pages 13–16)

2 tomatoes, peeled and chopped (page 21)

1 pound string beans

¾ cup boiling water

Coarse salt to taste

Heat the oil in a skillet and gently fry the onion with the garlic without browning. Add the chilies and fry for a couple of minutes. Add the tomatoes, the beans, and the water, bring to a boil, cover, and turn down the heat. Let the beans simmer gently until they are done (about 15 minutes), adding a little more water if you need it. Remove from heat, season with salt, and serve.

 SERVES 4

∿∿ STIR-FRIED SPICED CABBAGE ∿∿

**1 pound Chinese cabbage
(or green cabbage)**

2 tablespoons sugar

2 tablespoons vinegar

1 tablespoon soy sauce

**¼ to ½ teaspoon cayenne
pepper**

Coarse salt

**1 tablespoon peanut,
vegetable, or sesame oil**

2 cloves garlic, minced

**3 scallions, chopped
(including green part)**

Slice the cabbage fine. In a bowl, combine the sugar, vinegar, soy sauce, cayenne, and salt.

Heat the oil in a large skillet or wok. Add the garlic and scallions and stir-fry for 2 minutes. Add the cabbage and stir-fry for 2 to 3 minutes. Stir in the vinegar mixture, heat through, and remove from heat. Cool and serve at room temperature.

SERVES 4

CHILES RELLENOS

These stuffed peppers are made with *poblano* chilies, which are slightly smaller, darker, and much hotter than green peppers. The latter can be substituted but the taste is not the same at all.

The chilies should be held with a fork over a gas flame until the skin is charred and blistered. Wrap them in a dish towel and let stand for a few minutes. Peel the skin, slit them along the side, and remove the veins and seeds. If you use bell peppers, slice the top off and use it as a lid. Stuff the chilies with the stuffing mixture (see below) and secure the opening with a toothpick. You are then ready to dip them into the batter and fry them in hot oil.

〰〰 **CHILIES STUFFED WITH CHEESE** 〰〰

**8 2-by-4-inch slices
Monterey Jack or
mozzarella cheese**

**8 fresh green *poblano*
chilies, peeled (page 15)**

2 eggs, separated

½ teaspoon salt

Flour

**Peanut or vegetable oil
for frying**

**Salsa De Jitomate (page
246)**

Place a slice of cheese inside each chili. Beat the egg yolks lightly with the salt. Stiffly beat the egg whites until they stand in peaks. Dust the chilies with flour, then dip them into the yolks and then the whites. Fry the chilies in hot oil until golden brown all over. Do this in two batches. Drain on paper towels. Put the chilies in a casserole dish and bake in a preheated 375-degree oven for 20 minutes covered with the tomato sauce.

 SERVES 4

〰〰 **CHILIES STUFFED WITH BEANS** 〰〰

**8 fresh green *poblano*
chilies, peeled (page 15)**

**4 cups Mexican Refried
Beans (page 207)**

2 eggs, separated

½ teaspoon salt

Flour

**Peanut or vegetable oil
for frying**

¾ cup heavy cream

**6 ounces Cheddar cheese,
grated**

Stuff each chili with approximately ½ cup of the refried beans. Lightly beat the egg yolks with the salt. Stiffly beat the egg whites until they stand in peaks. Dust the chilies with flour, then dip them into the yolks and then the whites. Fry the chilies in hot oil until golden brown all over. Put in a casserole dish and cover with the cream and the cheese. Bake for about 20 minutes in a preheated 375-degree oven.

 SERVES 4

〰〰 CAULIFLOWER CHILI 〰〰

Serve this cauliflower with grilled meat or chicken and Mexican Beans (see page 206).

CAULIFLOWER

1 whole cauliflower
Water
½ cup grated cheddar cheese
2 tablespoons bread crumbs
Fresh chopped parsley or coriander to garnish

SAUCE

1 tablespoon peanut or vegetable oil
1 medium onion, chopped
2 cloves garlic, chopped
1 tablespoon Homemade Chili Powder (page 30)
3 tomatoes, peeled and chopped (page 21)
½ teaspoon ground cloves
Dash cinnamon
Coarse salt and freshly ground pepper to taste

To cook cauliflower, bring about an inch of water to a rolling boil, add cauliflower, and cook, covered, for about 10 minutes. Drain and reserve the water.

To cook sauce, heat the oil in a skillet and fry the onion with the garlic until soft. Add the chili powder, tomatoes, cloves, cinnamon, salt, and pepper. Cook together for about 5 minutes. Moisten with cauliflower water as necessary.

Arrange the cauliflower in a greased baking dish and spoon the sauce over it. Sprinkle with cheese and bread crumbs and bake in a preheated 350-degree oven for about 30 minutes. Sprinkle with parsley and serve.

 SERVES 6

∿∿ OKRA WITH CHILI AND CUMIN ∿∿

This is an Indian dish. Serve it along with rice and chicken, lamb, or fish dishes, or with curry.

1 pound okra
3 tablespoons *ghee* (page 38) or butter
1 medium onion, finely chopped
1 tablespoon ground cumin
1 tablespoon dried ground chilies (pages 13–16)
Coarse salt
Water

Wash the okra and trim off the ends. Heat the *ghee* in a skillet and gently fry the onion until golden without browning. Add the cumin and chili and fry for another minute. Pour in a little water, just enough to cover the bottom of the pan. Add okra and salt. Cover and cook over medium heat, stirring frequently, for about 20 minutes.

 SERVES 4

BALKAN MUSHROOMS
∿∿ WITH BLACK PEPPER ∿∿

Serve these mushrooms with noodles and a meat dish.

2 pounds mushrooms
1 medium onion, chopped
4 teaspoons butter
1 tablespoon freshly ground pepper
Coarse salt to taste
1 tablespoon fresh chopped dill
½ cup sour cream

Slice the mushrooms. Soften the onion in the butter in a frying pan and add the mushrooms. Grind on the pepper and add the salt and dill. Cook until the mushrooms are done, then add the cream. Heat through (do not boil) and serve.

 SERVES 4

〰 DEVILED TOMATOES 〰

Serve with steaks and grilled meat or seafood.

4 tomatoes, halved

1 clove garlic, finely chopped

Coarse salt and freshly ground pepper

Cayenne pepper

Bread crumbs

Olive oil

2 tablespoons butter

1 teaspoon Dijon mustard

Dash Worcestershire sauce

Dash Tabasco sauce

1 tablespoon red wine vinegar

1 teaspoon sugar

Fresh chopped parsley to garnish

Arrange the tomatoes on a broiling pan and sprinkle with garlic, salt, pepper, cayenne, bread crumbs, and olive oil. Broil for 10 to 15 minutes.

Meanwhile, in a small saucepan combine the remaining ingredients (except the parsley). Bring to a boil and set aside. Arrange the tomatoes on a dish and put a little sauce on each one. Sprinkle with parsley and serve.

 SERVES 4

〰 **FRIED GREEN TOMATOES** 〰

These are delicious with chicken, pork, or mackerel.

2 pounds green tomatoes
1 teaspoon Tabasco sauce
1 teaspoon soy sauce
1 teaspoon Worcestershire
sauce
1 cup flour
1 teaspoon cayenne
pepper
½ teaspoon chili powder
¼ teaspoon dry mustard
¼ teaspoon ground cumin
Coarse salt and freshly
ground pepper
Peanut or olive oil for
frying

Slice the tomatoes and marinate them in a mixture of the Tabasco, soy, and Worcestershire sauces for half an hour. Combine the remaining ingredients (except the oil) in a large bowl or plastic bag and coat the tomato slices. Heat enough oil to cover the bottom of a frying pan and fry the tomatoes until brown and crisp. Serve at once.

 SERVES 4

⋙ PAPRIKA ONIONS WITH YOGURT ⋘

A Balkan dish, this goes well with pork, veal, or chicken, accompanied by noodles.

4 large onions
4 ounces butter
Dash olive oil
¼ teaspoon ground mace
¼ teaspoon freshly grated nutmeg
1 tablespoon Hungarian paprika
½ tablespoon flour
1 cup plain yogurt
Coarse salt and freshly ground black pepper

Slice the onions and fry them in the butter with the oil, mace, nutmeg, and paprika until they are soft but not brown. Sprinkle on the flour and cook for 2 or 3 minutes, stirring. Add the yogurt, stir well, and heat through. Correct seasoning and serve.

 SERVES 4

〰〰 **INDIAN SPICED EGGPLANT** 〰〰

You can serve this with an Indian meal or with grilled meats such as lamb or chicken. It is an unusual, slightly sweet-sour dish and very good—one of the best ways I've eaten eggplant.

1 large eggplant

Coarse salt

4 tablespoons *ghee* (page 38) or butter

1½ tablespoons ground coriander

Freshly ground pepper

2 tablespoons sesame seeds

1 teaspoon paprika

Pinch asafetida

1-inch piece of fresh ginger, chopped

Juice of 1 lime or lemon

2 tablespoons chopped coriander to garnish

1 tablespoon chopped chives to garnish

Slice the eggplant, salt it, and let it stand for an hour. Heat 2 tablespoons of the *ghee* and fry the slices quickly on both sides. You may find that the eggplant soaks up the *ghee*—if so, add a little more, but not much or the dish will be too greasy. Simply dry-fry the slices to brown them. Set the eggplant aside. Fry the spices and ginger in remaining *ghee* and add the eggplant. Add the lime juice and cover. Simmer over very low heat until done, sprinkle with coriander and chives, and serve.

 SERVES 6

STARCH DISHES
〰〰〰

The recipes in this chapter are mainly accompaniments to spicy food. Each cuisine has its own particular way of cooking rice, noodles, beans, or potatoes and various kinds of breads to serve with a main course. Many of the dishes made from these ingredients are unusual and colorful—rice cooked with tomatoes and peppers, potatoes served with chilies and a cream sauce, beans and bananas mashed in a pancake, red and green *enchiladas*, and black beans combined with white rice, to name a few.

ENCHILADAS

Enchiladas are tortillas dipped in sauce, stuffed, rolled, and baked in the oven. They make excellent lunch dishes. You can stuff them with a variety of mixtures: cheese, cooked plantains, or leftover meat, chicken, or sausage. They are also very good with a *mole* sauce (see recipe for Turkey *Mole Poblano,* pages 142–143).

ᨄᨄ **RED ENCHILADAS** ᨄᨄ

6 *ancho* chilies, soaked in hot water for 30 minutes (page 15)

4 tomatoes, peeled and chopped (page 21)

2 medium onions, finely chopped

2 cloves garlic, chopped

½ teaspoon sugar

Coarse salt and freshly ground black pepper

2 eggs, lightly beaten

1 cup heavy cream

Lard or peanut oil

Sprig of *epazote*, if available

6 *chorizos*, skinned and chopped, (2 pounds ground meat or Italian hot sausage can be substituted)

12 tortillas

½ cup freshly grated Parmesan or cheddar cheese

Combine the chilies, tomatoes, 1 chopped onion (set remaining onion aside), garlic, sugar, salt, and pepper in a blender. Moisten with some of the chili-soaking liquid. Blend at high speed to a smooth purée. Mix eggs with cream. Heat 2 tablespoons lard or oil in a heavy skillet. Add the chili-tomato mixture with the *epazote* and cook for 5 minutes, stirring. Remove from heat, slowly stir in the egg and cream mixture. Set aside.

In another skillet fry the sausage meat and remove with slotted spoon. Add more lard or oil. Dip the tortillas into the sauce, then fry them very lightly in the fat, just enough to soften them. Don't fry too long or they will become hard. In each tortilla place a spoonful of the sausage meat. Roll them up and put them in an oven-proof dish. When you have filled the dish with the *enchiladas*, pour on the rest of the sauce and sprinkle with remaining chopped onion and grated cheese. Bake in a hot oven at 350 degrees for about 15 minutes.

 SERVES 6

∿∿ GREEN ENCHILADAS ∿∿

6 *poblano* chilies, skinned and chopped (page 15)

1 10-ounce can Mexican green tomatoes

¼ cup coarsely chopped fresh coriander

Coarse salt and freshly ground pepper

2 eggs, lightly beaten

1 cup heavy cream

3 whole chicken breasts, cooked and diced

6 ounces cream cheese

12 tortillas

3 tablespoons lard or peanut oil

¼ cup freshly grated Parmesan cheese

1 medium onion, finely chopped

Combine the chilies, green tomatoes, coriander, and salt and pepper in a blender with enough liquid from the tomatoes to make a thick purée. Mix eggs with the cream and add to the purée. Combine chicken and cream cheese and moisten with some of the sauce.

Dip the tortillas into the purée and fry in the lard or oil as in preceding recipe. Spread with chicken mixture, roll up, and place in ovenproof dish. Bring remaining sauce to a boil, pour over *enchiladas*, sprinkle with cheese and onions, and bake at 350 degrees for about 15 minutes in a hot oven.

🌑 SERVES 6

⋙ **MEXICAN BEANS** ⋙

Mexicans don't usually bother to soak the beans overnight. They leave them to simmer at the back of the stove until they are cooked, adding more water as needed and skimming off any foam that rises to the top. Beans accompany almost every meal and come in a variety of colors and sizes. The most common are *frijol negro* (black bean), *frijol pinto* (pinto bean), *frijol rojo* (kidney and California pink bean), and *frijol canario* (pale yellow bean).

Beans are particularly good with pork, spareribs, and chicken, accompanied by fried bananas. They should be fairly soupy. Do not use stale beans; they take almost forever to cook.

1 pound dried beans
Water to cover
1 medium onion, coarsely
    chopped
1 bay leaf
Coarse salt and freshly
    ground black pepper
1 small green fresh chili
    finely chopped (pages
    14–16)
Herb bouquet (parsley
    and thyme tied in
    cheesecloth)

Cover the beans with water in a large, heavy-bottomed casserole. Add the remaining ingredients and simmer, partially covered, until cooked, adding more water as needed.

 SERVES 4

∧∧∧ MEXICAN REFRIED BEANS ∧∧∧

Cook the beans according to Mexican Beans (see page 206). Canned beans may be used. They improve if you fry an onion, a garlic clove, and a chopped chili in the oil and mash them into the beans. For health reasons, peanut oil is preferable to lard or bacon fat.

½ recipe Mexican Beans (page 206)
Peanut oil, lard, or bacon fat

Mash the beans well with a fork. Heat the oil in a skillet. Add the beans and mash them in, stirring continuously. If you like, add some ground cumin, oregano, or crushed garlic. Add more oil and continue mashing, and when the beans are hot and sizzling and have become crisp underneath, turn them out and serve them.

❧ SERVES 4

∧∧∧ SERBIAN BEANS ∧∧∧

1 pound navy beans, soaked in water overnight
3 medium onions, coarsely chopped
½ pound smoked ham, cut into 1-inch cubes
Coarse salt and freshly ground pepper
1 tablespoon butter
1 tablespoon Hungarian paprika

Drain the beans and simmer in water to cover with 2 of the onions, the ham, and salt and pepper for about 2 hours. Fry the remaining onion in the butter and add the paprika. Cook for a minute and add to the beans. Cook for 10 minutes. Correct seasoning and serve.

❧ SERVES 4

ᢥᢤᢥ YUGOSLAV PAPRIKA POTATOES ᢥᢤᢥ

Serve these with chicken, pork or veal chops, steak or a roast. The only other vegetable you will need is a green salad.

2 pounds potatoes
2 medium onions
1 tablespoon peanut or vegetable oil
2 tablespoons butter
2 tablespoons Hungarian paprika
½ cup sour cream
Coarse salt to taste
Pimiento strips and chopped parsley to garnish

Boil the potatoes until done. Meanwhile, chop the onions and fry gently until soft in the oil and butter. Add the paprika and continue cooking for 2 minutes, being careful to prevent burning. Set aside.

Mash the potatoes and mix in the onions and the sour cream. Season with salt and put the mixture in a buttered baking dish. Dot with butter and sprinkle on a little paprika and brown under a broiler. Garnish with pimiento and parsley and serve.

 SERVES 4

ᢥᢤᢥ PERUVIAN SWEET POTATOES ᢥᢤᢥ

These baked potatoes are excellent with pork chops or spareribs, turkey or chicken. A green vegetable would be a good accompaniment.

6 sweet potatoes, baked in their skins
4 ounces cream cheese
1 egg yolk
1 teaspoon chili powder

Mash the flesh from the sweet potatoes, reserving the skins. Add the remaining ingredients except the butter and stuff back into the skins. Dot with butter, sprinkle with extra chili

3 scallions, chopped

Coarse salt and freshly
  ground pepper to taste

Butter

powder, and quickly brown on a hot grill or under a broiler.

❧ SERVES 6

JAVANESE POTATOES
 WITH TAMARIND SAUCE

Prepared in advance, the potatoes can be kept hot in the oven in their sauce. Serve them with other Indonesian and Southeast Asian dishes, or with chicken or meat.

1 red or green bell
  pepper, chopped

1 medium onion, chopped

1 clove garlic, chopped

2 tablespoons peanut or
  vegetable oil

½ cup Tamarind Water
  (page 35)

1 tablespoon dark brown
  sugar

½-inch piece of fresh
  ginger, chopped

¼ teaspoon *trassi* (page 9)

Coarse salt

4 medium-size potatoes

Oil for deep frying

Fry the pepper, onion, and garlic in the peanut oil until soft. Add the tamarind water, sugar, and ginger. Mix well, add the *trassi* and salt. Bring to a boil and simmer until the liquid has reduced to a thick paste. Set aside.

Cut the potatoes into thin slices and deep-fry until golden. Drain on paper towels. Combine with the sauce and serve hot.

❧ SERVES 4

∿∿ **INDIAN POTATO FRITTERS** ∿∿

Leftover potatoes can be used. These go with most chicken and meat dishes, stews, roasts, or grilled meat.

1 cup mashed potatoes

3 eggs

1 finely minced green chili (page 14–16)

2 tablespoons chopped onion or scallion

2 tablespoons milk

Coarse salt and freshly ground pepper

Freshly grated nutmeg

½ teaspoon baking powder

½ teaspoon cumin seed

½ teaspoon ground mustard seed

2 tablespoons *ghee* (page 38) or peanut oil

Mix the mashed potatoes with the remaining ingredients except the *ghee*. Shape the mixture into patties about 2½ inches in diameter. Fry in hot *ghee* and drain on paper towels. Use more *ghee* if necessary.

✿ **SERVES 4**

∿ **RICE** ∿

It is important not to overcook rice. It should be tested after 12 minutes of cooking. The grains should be soft without being either mushy or hard in the center.

The popular brands of rice available in supermarkets are not as good as Indian Patna rice or Italian rice. Instant rice is worthless. Use Patna for boiled rice dishes. The grain is thinner and absorbs less water. Italian rice is good for *risotto* because it absorbs more liquid.

∿ **RICE 1** ∿

Water

Salt

⅓ to ½ cup rice per person

Butter

Half-fill a large pot with water, salt it, and bring to a boil. Add the rice gradually so that the water does not stop boiling. Stir with a fork and boil the rice rapidly, uncovered. Test after 12 minutes. It usually takes 15 to 20 minutes. When done, empty the rice into a colander and run under cold water. Melt some butter in a separate saucepan, add the rice, cover with a cloth, and leave for a few minutes (or up to half an hour). Alternatively you can melt some butter in a baking dish and put the rice into a warm oven until needed.

NOTE: Half a lemon added to the boiling water keeps the rice white. Oil added prevents it from boiling over.

∿∿ RICE 2 ∿∿

1 tablespoon butter
1 teaspoon salt
2½ cups water
1 cup rice

Put butter in salted water and bring to a boil. Add rice gradually, cover, and reduce flame to low. Simmer for about 20 minutes, or until done. Use a tight-fitting cover.

∿∿ PLAIN BOILED RICE, CHINESE-STYLE ∿∿

1 cup long-grain rice
1¾ cups cold water

Rinse rice under cold water. Put into a 2-quart saucepan and add the cold water. Bring to a boil. Stir, and when it reaches a rolling boil, cover tightly, reduce heat to low, and cook for 20 minutes. Turn off heat and let rice stand for 10 minutes. Serve hot.

 SERVES 2

∿∿ SAFFRON RICE, CARIBBEAN-STYLE ∿∿

1 medium onion, chopped
3 tablespoons olive oil
1½ cups rice
Pinch saffron
2½ cups Chicken Stock
   (page 42)
Coarse salt

Fry the onion in the oil until golden. Add the rice and saffron and fry for 5 minutes. Boil the stock, add it, and season with salt. Stir and cook over low heat for 15 to 20 minutes, covered. Stir occasionally.

 SERVES 4

ᗯᗯ ARROZ À LA MEXICANA ᗯᗯ

MEXICAN RICE

This is good with Mexican dishes or grilled fish, meat, or chicken.

1 medium onion, coarsely chopped
2 cloves garlic, peeled
4 cups chicken stock
4 ripe tomatoes, peeled and chopped (page 21)
¼ cup olive oil
2 cups white rice
1 cup peas (if frozen peas are used, they should first be thawed)
Coarse salt and freshly ground pepper
4 to 5 red and green fresh chili peppers (pages 13–16)
Fresh coriander
1 avocado
Fresh lemon or lime juice

Put the onion and the garlic in a blender with ½ cup of the chicken stock and the tomatoes. Blend until smooth.

Heat the oil in a large saucepan. Fry the rice until opaque. Add the tomato mixture, peas, and the remaining stock. Season with salt and pepper. Simmer, covered, until nearly all the liquid is absorbed.

Cut the chilies from tip down to stem in strips so that they form flowers. Garnish the rice with the chilies, coriander sprigs, and peeled and sliced avocado on which you have squeezed lemon or lime juice to prevent it from turning brown.

 SERVES 6

∿∿∿ ARROZ VERDE ∿∿∿

MEXICAN GREEN RICE

Serve with Mexican food, chicken, fish, and grilled meats. Bell peppers plus a teaspoon of ground dried chilies may be substituted for *poblano* chilies.

4 cups Chicken Stock (page 42)

4 *poblano* chilies, peeled and coarsely chopped (page 15)

1 cup chopped fresh parsley or coriander

1 medium onion, coarsely chopped

1 clove garlic, peeled

Coarse salt and freshly ground pepper

¼ cup olive oil

2 cups long-grain rice

Combine ½ cup of the stock and remaining ingredients except oil and rice in a blender. Reduce to a smooth purée. Set aside.

Pour oil in heavy casserole and when hot add the rice. Stir until the grains become opaque. Add the chili mixture and the remaining stock, which you have brought to a boil in a separate pan. Simmer for about 20 minutes, or until rice has absorbed all the liquid.

 **SERVES 4 TO 6**

ᗩᗩᗩ PEAS AND RICE ᗩᗩᗩ

This always looks attractive and can be served with any curry or main dish.

2 medium onions, chopped

2 tablespoons *ghee* (page 38) or butter

1 tablespoon cardamom seeds

2-inch cinnamon stick

1½ cups long grain or basmati rice

1 pound peas (podded fresh or frozen)

4 cups boiling water

Fry the onions in the *ghee* without browning. Add the cardamom seeds, cinnamon, and rice. Fry for 7 minutes. Add the peas and cook for 3 minutes, stirring constantly to prevent burning. Add the water and cook, covered, for about 30 minutes, or until rice is done.

 SERVES 4 TO 6

ᗩᗩᗩ KITCHIRI ᗩᗩᗩ

RICE AND LENTILS

This is a traditional accompaniment for curries. A bowl of yogurt and a bowl of lemon or mango pickles go well with it.

3 cups long-grain or basmati rice

½ pound lentils

Coarse salt

6 cups water

4 tablespoons *ghee* (page 38) or butter

½ tablespoon cumin seed

Rinse the rice and the lentils and cook in boiling salted water until soft. Drain thoroughly. Melt the *ghee*, stir in the cumin seed, and pour the mixture over the rice and lentils.

SERVES 6

ᗯᗯ **MOORS AND CHRISTIANS** ᗯᗯ

CUBAN BLACK BEANS AND RICE

Leftover black beans can be used for this recipe (see page 206 for Mexican Beans).

2 tablespoons olive oil
1 clove garlic, chopped
1 medium onion, chopped
1 green bell pepper,
chopped
1½ cups long-grain white
rice
2 cups water
2 cups cooked black beans
Coarse salt and freshly
ground pepper

Heat the oil in a heavy saucepan and fry the garlic, onion, and pepper until soft but not brown. Add the rice, fry for a couple of minutes until opaque, add the water, beans, and seasonings. Cover and simmer over low heat until all the water has been absorbed (about 20 minutes).

🌶 SERVES 4

ᗯᗯ **BHUGIA** ᗯᗯ

Served with Indian meals, these are golden puffs, rather like doughnuts in appearance but without the hole in the middle. Make the batter in advance and cook them at the last minute so that they are hot when served.

1 cup plain white flour
1 teaspoon turmeric
¼ teaspoon dried ground
chilies (pages 13–16)
2 scallions, minced
2 fresh chilies, minced
(pages 13–16)
2 eggs

Mix the flour with the turmeric, ground chili, scallions, chilies, and add the eggs. Mix well, season with salt and pepper, and if too dry moisten with a little milk. Stir in the vegetables.

**Coarse salt and freshly
  ground pepper**
Milk to moisten
**¼ cup chopped cooked
  vegetables (peas, carrot,
  cauliflower, etc.)**
Oil for deep frying

Heat oil in a deep-fryer and when hot drop the batter in by tablespoons. Drain on paper and keep hot.

❧ SERVES 4 TO 6

⋀⋁⋀ CHAPATTIS ⋀⋁⋀

These Indian breads are easy to make and go well with curry. Leave the dough for half an hour in a warm place before you roll it out.

**2 cups whole-wheat flour
  (do not use white)**
**2 tablespoons *ghee* (page
  38)**
Pinch salt
**½ to 1 cup water
  (approximately)**

Mix the flour, *ghee,* and salt. Put the mixture on a pastry board and make a well in the middle. Add the water, a little at a time, until dough becomes elastic, and knead until smooth (5 to 10 minutes). Cover with a damp cloth and allow dough to rest for half an hour.

Knead the dough lightly, mold it into small balls (about 1½ inches in diameter), and roll out as thin as possible. Dust with flour. Heat a heavy-bottomed skillet or griddle (with no fat in it) and fry the *chapattis* for two minutes on each side. When the bread puffs up it is ready. Serve with butter or *ghee,* (see page 38).

❧ YIELD: ABOUT 12 5-INCH CHAPATTIS

∿∿ SAMOSA ∿∿

INDIAN PASTRY TURNOVER

These turnovers are delicious hot or cold (better hot) and can be served as an appetizer or with a main course. You can vary the stuffing. Most common is a mixture of mashed potatoes, chopped green peas, chopped chives, parsley, and mint, paprika, and salt moistened with lime juice. Ground beef or lamb that has been cooked with garlic and onions and flavored with chopped parsley, mint, and chives is also popular.

4 cups plain white flour

4 tablespoons *ghee* (page 38) or butter

¾ tablespoon salt

Yogurt or sour milk as needed to make a dough

Stuffing (see paragraph above)

Oil for deep frying

Sift the flour and work in the melted *ghee*. Season with salt, knead in the yogurt, beginning with about ½ cup, until you have a stiff but pliable dough. Shape into small balls and roll out into circles about 2 inches in diameter. Place a spoonful of stuffing in each circle, wet the edges and roll over the other half, press down, and deep-fry in oil until golden. Drain on paper towels.

🌶 **SERVES 6 TO 8**

ᗯᗯ HUNGARIAN EGG DUMPLINGS ᗯᗯ

Serve these with Székely Gulyás (see page 156) or Hungarian Veal Paprikash (see page 167).

1½ cups all-purpose flour

3 tablespoons coarse salt

2 eggs

½ cup milk

1 stick butter, melted

About 2 quarts boiling water

Sift the flour into a bowl with the salt. Beat the eggs and add with the milk and 1 tablespoon of the melted butter. Mix thoroughly so that there are no lumps. Drop a spoonful at a time into the boiling water and cook until the dumplings rise to the surface (about 8 to 10 minutes). Drain thoroughly, put in a warm bowl, and pour remaining melted butter over them. Keep warm until ready to serve.

 SERVES 4

ᗯᗯ DAL ᗯᗯ

This Indian lentil dish should have the consistency of thick sauce.

1 pound lentils

½ teaspoon turmeric

½ teaspoon chili powder

2 medium onions, chopped

1 tablespoon *ghee* (page 38) or butter

4 tomatoes, peeled and chopped (page 21)

Coarse salt and freshly ground pepper

Simmer the lentils in water to cover with the turmeric and chili powder. Meanwhile, cook the onion in the *ghee* and add the tomatoes. Simmer gently for about 10 minutes.

Add the tomato-onion mixture to the cooked lentils, season with salt and pepper, and serve.

 SERVES 4

〰️ JALAPEÑO CORN BREAD 〰️

Serve with Mexican food or with grilled meat or fish.

2½ cups yellow cornmeal
1 cup white flour
2 tablespoons sugar
1 tablespoon coarse salt
4 tablespoons baking
powder
3 eggs
1½ cups milk
½ cup peanut oil
2 cups canned creamed
corn
8 *jalapeño* chilies,
chopped (pages 14–15)
2 cups grated sharp
cheddar cheese
1 medium onion, grated

Combine the cornmeal, flour, sugar, salt, and baking powder in a mixing bowl. Beat the eggs, add the milk, peanut oil, and stir in the creamed corn. Add the chilies, cheese, and onion. Stir into the flour mixture and pour into 2 oiled 9-by-11-inch pans. Bake in a preheated 425-degree oven until done (about 25 minutes).

 **YIELD: 2 LOAVES**

SALADS

Salad is usually best served after, not before, the main course. There are, however, certain mixed salads that are good as hors d'oeuvres. This chapter contains several such salads, raw or cooked, all of them spicy, that are also excellent lunch dishes. They are interesting in buffet spreads too.

Plain green salads and light salads to be served after spicy foods are also included here. The freshest, ripest ingredients should be used. Vegetables should be washed and dried with dishcloths unless they are organically grown and clean. Lettuce should be torn into strips, other vegetables chopped the same size. Bottled dressings are an anathema.

GREEN SALAD
〰〰 WITH VINAIGRETTE DRESSING 〰〰

Fresh green leafy vegetables only should be used in this salad. These may include lettuce, spinach leaves, endive, watercress, dandelion leaves, arugula, young escarole, diced fennel, green bell peppers, or thinly sliced cucumbers. Fresh green herbs such as basil, mint, tarragon, chives, parsley, or coriander are excellent— but dried herbs won't do.

A basic dressing is the vinaigrette, which should be poured over the salad shortly before serving. Combine 2 tablespoons tarragon or red wine vinegar with 6 tablespoons extra virgin olive oil, ¼ teaspoon Dijon mustard, 1 crushed garlic clove (if you like), coarse salt, and freshly ground black pepper. Proportions will vary according to the sharpness of the vinegar. Toss the salad thoroughly, correct seasoning, let stand for a minute or two, and then serve.

᭡᭡᭡ RICE SALAD ᭡᭡᭡

This salad is good with spicy grilled meat or fish.

3 cups hot cooked rice

4 tomatoes, peeled and chopped (page 21)

2 green bell peppers, chopped

1 diced fresh green or red chili, chopped (pages 13–16)

1 tablespoon chopped fresh parsley, chives, or coriander

Other ingredients according to taste:

Chopped bottled pimientos

Diced raw mushrooms

Cooked green peas

Chopped olives

Chopped cucumber

Chopped hard-boiled egg

Paprika

Combine the rice with a vinaigrette dressing (see under Green Salad with Vinaigrette Dressing, page 223) and add the remaining ingredients. Toss, cool, and serve at room temperature.

 SERVES 4

ᗭᗢᗢᗢ KIM CHEE ᗢᗢᗢ

KOREAN PICKLED CABBAGE

Kim chee is Korea's national dish. It is very good with broiled or stir-fried meats and chicken. Rice is the other side dish to serve along with this pickled cabbage.

Chinese cabbage is available in many supermarkets nowadays, besides Chinese and specialty stores. *Kim chee* can also be bought canned.

1 head Chinese cabbage

2 tablespoons coarse salt

4 scallions

1 clove garlic

2 hot chilies, finely chopped (pages 13–16)

Dash Tabasco sauce

½-inch piece of fresh ginger, grated

Chop the cabbage coarsely and salt it. Let stand for an hour, then rinse it under cold water to remove the salt.

Shred the scallions, mince the garlic, and add to the cabbage with the chilies, Tabasco, and ginger. Place the mixture in a glass or earthenware jar and add water to cover. Leave for 1 to 5 days in the lower part of the refrigerator. Serve at room temperature. *Kim chee* can be stored in a sealed jar in the refrigerator.

 SERVES 8

MOROCCAN FENNEL SALAD

1 pound fennel hearts
¼ teaspoon ground cumin
½ teaspoon paprika
¼ cup olive oil
Juice of half a lemon
1 teaspoon prepared
**   mustard**
Coarse salt and freshly
**   ground pepper**

Slice the fennel into very thin rounds. Combine the remaining ingredients, correct seasoning, and pour onto the fennel. Toss and serve.

❧ **SERVES 4**

NOTE: Moroccan salads are generally served at the beginning of a meal.

BEAN SPROUT SALAD
WITH MUSTARD DRESSING

Serve this salad with Chinese meals or with broiled chicken, fish, or meat.

1 pound fresh bean
**   sprouts**
Boiling water
1 tablespoon dry mustard
2 tablespoons soy sauce
1 teaspoon sugar
2 tablespoons white wine
**   vinegar or cider vinegar**
½ cup sesame or mustard
**   oil**

Wash the bean sprouts and pour boiling water over them. Drain. Set aside.

Combine the remaining ingredients and pour the mixture on the bean sprouts. Toss well and let stand for an hour before serving.

❧ **SERVES 4**

NOTE: This mustard dressing is very good with cold chicken. Use half the amount of oil.

〰〰 ASINAN 〰〰

INDONESIAN VEGETABLE SALAD

VEGETABLES

½ pound fresh bean
  sprouts, steamed for 1
  minute

½ pound shredded green
  cabbage

1 cucumber, thinly sliced

1 bunch radishes, thinly
  sliced

1 1-pound bean curd,
  cubed

1 cup chopped roasted
  unsalted peanuts

DRESSING

3 hot fresh chilies, minced
  (pages 13–16)

½ teaspoon minced fresh
  ginger

1 clove garlic, finely
  chopped

2 tablespoons sugar

¼ cup vinegar

2 cups water

½ teaspoon *trassi* (page 9)

Coarse salt and freshly
  ground pepper

Arrange vegetables in a mound on a large plate.

To make the dressing, mix the chilies, ginger, garlic, sugar, and vinegar in an electric blender until it forms a smooth purée. Add the water and the *trassi* and blend for a few seconds more. Season with salt and pepper. Pour over the salad and serve.

❧ SERVES 4

᭐᭐᭐ GADO GADO ᭐᭐᭐

COOKED INDONESIAN VEGETABLE SALAD

The vegetables should be slightly crisp after steaming. Do not overcook them.

VEGETABLES

- **2 1-pound bean curd cakes, cubed and deep-fried in peanut oil until crisp**
- **6 small new potatoes, cooked**
- **1 pound string beans, steamed**
- **1 pound spinach, steamed**
- **1 pound bean sprouts, blanched**
- **2 cucumbers, thinly sliced, with skins (unless the skins have been paraffin waxed)**
- **2 hard-boiled eggs**

SAUCE

- **3 tablespoons peanut oil**
- **1 medium onion, chopped**
- **3 cloves garlic, chopped**
- **1 teaspoon *trassi* (page 9)**
- **2 fresh chilies, coarsely chopped (pages 13–16)**

Arrange vegetables on a platter.

To make sauce, heat the oil in a deep, heavy-bottomed frying pan. Cook the onions and garlic for 5 minutes without burning. Add the *trassi*, blend, and put the mixture in a blender with the chilies and peanuts. Blend at high speed, using a little coconut milk to moisten if necessary. Add the *laos* powder, ginger, remaining coconut milk, sugar, and tamarind water. Blend until smooth. Return to skillet. Bring to a boil and simmer for about 15 minutes, or until sauce is consistency of heavy cream. Add salt and lemon juice, correct the seasoning, and pour over the vegetables. Garnish with chopped scallions if you like. The sauce may be also be served separately in a sauceboat.

 **SERVES 6 TO 8**

4 cups roasted unsalted
   peanuts

4 cups Coconut Milk
   (pages 36–37)

½ teaspoon *laos* powder
   (page 9)

1 teaspoon minced fresh
   ginger

3 tablespoons brown
   sugar

¼ cup Tamarind Water
   (page 35)

Coarse salt to taste

Lemon juice to taste

Chopped scallions to
   garnish (optional)

⌇⌇⌇ YOGURT CUCUMBER SALAD ⌇⌇⌇

A very cooling salad to serve with hot curries. It can be eaten separately or together with a curry.

2 cucumbers

Coarse salt

½ cup plain yogurt

1 tablespoon vinegar or
   lemon juice

1 clove garlic, chopped

Freshly ground pepper

Fresh chopped mint or
   basil

Peel the cucumbers and slice thinly. Salt them and let stand for about half an hour. Squeeze out the excess moisture with paper towels. Combine the yogurt, vinegar, garlic, and pepper and toss the cucumber in this mixture. Correct seasoning, sprinkle with herbs, and chill until ready to eat.

 SERVES 4

〰〰 TURKISH CUCUMBERS IN YOGURT 〰〰

This salad is an antidote to hot, spicy dishes.

2 cucumbers
Coarse salt
1 cup plain yogurt
2 cloves garlic, minced
Freshly ground black
pepper
1 tablespoon fresh
chopped dill or mint
(optional)

Peel the cucumbers and slice thinly. Salt them and let them stand for half an hour. Pat them dry with paper towels. Mix the yogurt with garlic, pepper, and dill. Correct seasoning and pour over the cucumbers. Toss well and serve chilled.

🐝 **SERVES 4**

〰〰 MUSTARD SPINACH SALAD 〰〰

This is a good salad to serve after lamb or chicken dishes.

1 pound young spinach
½ cup olive oil
2 tablespoons Dijon
mustard
3 tablespoons red wine
vinegar
½ Spanish onion, finely
chopped
Squeeze of lemon juice to
taste
Coarse salt and freshly
ground pepper

Wash the spinach thoroughly in several changes of water. Remove tough stems, dry the leaves well, and refrigerate until ready to use.

Combine the oil with the remaining ingredients and mix well. Pour the dressing over the spinach, toss, and serve.

🐝 **SERVES 4**

MOROCCAN GREEN PEPPER
〰〰 AND TOMATO SALAD 〰〰

Don't bother to make this if you can't get ripe, juicy tomatoes.

4 tomatoes, (page 21)

3 green bell peppers, (page 21)

1 tablespoon chopped fresh green chilies (pages 14–16)

3 tablespoons olive oil

½ teaspoon ground cumin

Coarse salt and freshly ground pepper

Juice of 1 lemon

½ Moroccan Preserved Lemon (page 260)

2 tablespoons chopped parsley

Arrange the vegetables and chopped chilies in a dish. Combine the oil, cumin, salt, pepper and lemon juice and pour over. Chop the skin of the preserved lemon, sprinkle on the vegetables along with the parsley. Serve at room temperature.

❧ SERVES 4

SAALOUK

MOROCCAN EGGPLANT SALAD

This salad is like a spicy *ratatouille* and should be served as an appetizer.

2 pounds eggplant

3 zucchini

Olive oil for frying

2 green bell peppers (page 21)

2 small fresh green chilies (pages 14–16)

3 tomatoes, peeled, seeded, and diced (page 21)

3 cloves garlic

2 teaspoons ground cumin

1 teaspoon paprika

2 tablespoons fresh chopped coriander

Coarse salt and freshly ground pepper

Juice of 1 lime or lemon

Cut the eggplant into slices ½-inch thick, salt, and let drain in a colander for 30 minutes. Slice the zucchini. Heat the oil in a heavy frying pan and fry the eggplant and zucchini until lightly browned. Remove with a slotted spoon and reserve the oil.

Mash the eggplant and zucchini with the bell peppers, chilies, tomatoes, garlic, cumin, paprika, coriander, salt, pepper, and lemon juice. Add the reserved oil. Correct the seasoning. Serve at room temperature.

 SERVES 4

MIDDLE EASTERN
〰️ CHICK-PEA SALAD 〰️

The effort and time required to cook dried chick-peas is hardly worth it; the canned ones are very good, but they should be rinsed thoroughly and heated to absorb the dressing.

This is a good salad to serve with lamb, curries, and Indian meals. It can also be served on lettuce leaves with tomatoes, peppers, pimientos, and celery.

**3 cups cooked chick-peas
  (or 2 10-ounce cans)
Water
½ cup olive oil
3 tablespoons vinegar
Lemon juice to taste
Coarse salt and freshly
  ground pepper
1 clove garlic, finely
  chopped (optional)
1 medium onion, chopped
1 cup chopped vegetables
  (celery, tomatoes,
  peppers, or all three)
2 tablespoons diced
  pimientos
Fresh chopped parsley to
  garnish**

Rinse the chick-peas, heat them in some water, and drain. Mix the oil with the vinegar, lemon juice, salt, and pepper. Add the garlic and the onions and toss the warm chick-peas thoroughly with the mixture. Add the vegetables, mix in, and arrange the pimientos on top of the salad. Sprinkle with parsley.

❧ SERVES 4

PAPRIKA SALAD
∾∾∾ WITH LEMON DRESSING ∾∾∾

SALAD

2 tart apples
2 stalks celery
1 orange
1 cup halved, shelled
walnuts
1 head Boston lettuce

DRESSING

Juice of half a lemon
¼ teaspoon grated lemon
peel
½ teaspoon dry mustard
1 tablespoon dark
prepared mustard
1 tablespoon Hungarian
paprika
¼ cup walnut oil
Coarse salt
½ cup heavy cream

To make the salad, peel and chop the apples. Chop the celery, peel and chop the orange, and combine in a salad bowl with the walnuts. Wash and dry the lettuce, tear into strips, and add.

To make the dressing, combine all the dressing ingredients (except the cream) in a bowl. Little by little, beat the cream into the dressing. Pour over the salad, toss, and serve.

 SERVES 4

SAUCES &
MARINADES

A n ordinary piece of meat or fish can be transformed by its sauce. Sauces are extremely important in hot, spicy cuisines. Some may be "on the table" sauces that can be made and kept in a sealed jar under refrigeration for about a week, sometimes longer. Others are freshly made. See the chapter on relishes for Indonesian *sambals,* which are a distant relative of Mexican table sauces.

Cold sauces can be set out in small bowls or used as dips. They are delicious with cold meat.

This chapter also has a section on marinades that will make meat more tender and improve its taste. Meat can be kept for up to a week in a marinade. (Indians say meat marinated in mustard oil will keep for months but I haven't tried it.) Even fish can be kept for a couple of days in a marinade, at room temperature in cool weather. By using a marinade you can avoid freezing meat and fish, and enhance their flavor.

SAUCES

⋀⋀⋁ DEVIL SAUCE ⋁⋀⋀

4 tablespoons butter

2 shallots, chopped

2 green chilies, chopped
(pages 14–16)

1 tablespoon fresh ginger,
chopped

2 cups homemade stock
(beef or chicken)

1 cup red wine

1 tablespoon red wine
vinegar

2 tablespoons mango
chutney

1 tablespoon red currant
jelly

Melt the butter in a saucepan and cook the shallots, chilies, and ginger until the shallots are soft. Add the stock and wine and bring to a boil. Season with remaining ingredients and serve with tongue or ham.

❧ **YIELD: ABOUT 2½ CUPS**

⋀⋀⋁ MUSTARD SAUCE ⋁⋀⋀

Good with fish, ham, and pork.

1 tablespoon butter

1 tablespoon olive oil

1 medium onion, finely
chopped

Parsley sprigs

Heat butter and oil in a saucepan. Add onion and parsley and fry until onion is soft, without browning. Sprinkle with flour, cook, stirring, for 2 minutes. Add stock and wine and

1 tablespoon flour
1 cup fish, chicken, or
    meat stock
1 cup dry white wine
3 tablespoons Dijon
    mustard
Coarse salt and freshly
    ground pepper

bring to a boil. Simmer for about 20 minutes.

Strain the sauce into the top of a double boiler. Add the mustard, stir well, and cook until thick and smooth. Season with salt and pepper.

❧ YIELD: ABOUT 2 CUPS

ᗯᗯEGG AND MUSTARD SAUCE FOR HAM ᗯᗯ

The trick to making this French sauce is to use a double boiler or a trivet. If it gets too hot, the eggs will curdle and your sauce will be ruined. Serve the sauce either separately with baked country ham or over ham slices.

3 eggs
2 tablespoons white wine
½ cup sour cream
2 teaspoons Dijon mustard
Coarse salt and freshly
    ground white pepper

Beat the eggs until thick and whip with a wire whisk in a small saucepan (or top of double boiler). Beat in the wine. Over low heat, add the sour cream gradually, beating constantly, and add the mustard. Season with salt and pepper, and when heated through and smooth remove from heat and serve immediately.

❧ YIELD: ABOUT 1 CUP

∿∿ SAUCE DIJONNAISE ∿∿

For cold fish, especially cold salmon.

4 hard-boiled eggs
5 tablespoons Dijon
mustard
Coarse salt and freshly
ground white pepper
1 cup olive oil
Juice of 1 lemon
1 tablespoon chopped
capers
1 tablespoon chopped
fresh chives
1 tablespoon chopped
fresh tarragon
Dash paprika

Sieve the egg yolks and set the whites aside. Combine the yolks with the mustard and season with salt and pepper. Beat together and then add the oil, drop by drop, beating it in as for a mayonnaise. Beat in the lemon juice, then add the remaining ingredients. To serve, spread over the fish and decorate with chopped egg whites and paprika.

 **YIELD: ABOUT 1½ CUPS**

∿∿ SOFRITO ∿∿

PUERTO RICO

The Spaniards brought this to the Caribbean, where it is now used as a basic cooking sauce. It can be made in large quantities and keeps for several weeks refrigerated, for several months frozen.

½ pound salt pork, finely diced

2 tablespoons *Achiote* Oil (page 34) or 1 tablespoon *annatto* seeds

4 medium onions, finely chopped

4 cloves garlic, finely chopped

2 green bell peppers, finely chopped

½ pound lean boneless ham, diced

4 tomatoes, coarsely chopped

1 tablespoon fresh coriander, chopped

1 teaspoon oregano

Coarse salt and freshly ground black pepper

Fry the salt pork in a heavy skillet. Remove with slotted spoon. Add the oil. If using seeds, fry them in the pork fat for 5 minutes, then remove. Add onions, garlic, and peppers and cook, stirring frequently, for 5 minutes. Add the ham, tomatoes, coriander, oregano, salt, and pepper. Stir and simmer, covered, for 20 minutes. Correct seasoning and store in tightly covered jars.

❧ YIELD: ABOUT 2 CUPS

∿∿ SAUCE CREOLE ∿∿

MARTINIQUE

This is delicious with broiled fish, crayfish, or lobster. It keeps for a week.

1 cup tomato purée
Juice of 2 limes
1 medium onion, finely chopped
1 tablespoon chopped celery
1 *serrano* chili, chopped (page 15)
4 pimiento-stuffed olives, sliced
Coarse salt and freshly ground pepper

Combine all ingredients in a bowl. Serve at once or cover tightly and store in refrigerator.

✍ YIELD: 1½ CUPS

〰️ SPICY TOMATO SAUCE 〰️

Use on pasta or with chicken or fish.

1 tablespoon olive oil
1 tablespoon butter
2 cloves garlic, finely
chopped
8 large ripe tomatoes,
peeled and chopped
(page 21)
1 teaspoon hot pepper
flakes (or to taste)
1 teaspoon sugar
Coarse salt and freshly
ground pepper
Freshly grated nutmeg

Melt the oil and butter in a saucepan and fry the garlic for 2 minutes without burning. Add the remaining ingredients and simmer until you have a thick purée, stirring frequently.

✥ **YIELD: 1½ CUPS**

〰️ SALSA VERDE 〰️

Use as a dipping sauce for tortillas, to enliven soups and beans, or as a table sauce with meat, fish, and eggs. It also goes with *Tacos*, (see page 56–57), *Enchiladas* (see pages 203–205), and *Panuchos* (see page 64).

½ pound Mexican green
tomatoes
2 cloves garlic, peeled
1 onion, coarsely chopped
2 green chilies, preferably
serrano (page 15)
½ cup coarsely chopped
coriander leaves
Coarse salt to taste

Combine all the ingredients in the jar of a blender and purée. Do not overblend, or the sauce will turn into a characterless frothy liquid.

✥ **YIELD: ABOUT 1½ CUPS**

∿∿ SALSA CRUDA ∿∿

This sauce appears on the table in Mexico to be served on the side with eggs for breakfast, with roasted or grilled meat or fish, on *tacos,* and on beans. In Yucatán, Seville orange juice is added. You can use regular fresh orange juice with a dash of lemon or lime juice to make it tart.

1 medium ripe tomato

1 small onion

3 green chilies, preferably *serrano* **(page 15)**

½ cup fresh coriander leaves

⅓ cup Seville orange juice (or regular juice with a dash of lemon or lime juice)

Chop all the ingredients finely (the chili is added seeds and all) and place in a small bowl and mix with orange juice. Season with salt to taste. Serve immediately.

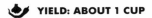 **YIELD: ABOUT 1 CUP**

〜〜 SALSA DE CHILE ROJO 〜〜

RED CHILI SAUCE

This is the classic Mexican sauce that is served on the side with most meals.

5 *ancho* chilies, fresh or dried, soaked for 30 minutes in 1 cup boiling water (page 13)

3 *pequín* chilies, crumbled (page 14)

3 tomatoes, peeled and chopped (page 21)

1 medium onion, coarsely chopped

1 clove garlic, peeled

¼ cup olive or peanut oil

Coarse salt and freshly ground pepper

½ teaspoon sugar

2 tablespoons chopped fresh coriander or parsley

1 tablespoon red wine vinegar

Combine chilies, tomatoes, onion, and garlic in a blender and blend to purée. Heat oil in a skillet and pour in the sauce. Season with salt and pepper; add sugar and coriander. Cook for 5 minutes, stirring. Remove from heat, stir in vinegar, and cool. Will keep for 4 to 5 days in the refrigerator.

🌂 **YIELD: 2 CUPS**

〰〰 SALSA DE JITOMATE 〰〰

MEXICAN COOKED TOMATO SAUCE

2 tablespoons peanut or
  vegetable oil
1 medium onion, finely
  chopped
1 clove garlic, finely
  chopped
4 large ripe tomatoes,
  peeled and chopped
  (page 21)
2 *serrano* chilies, chopped
  (page 15)
Coarse salt and freshly
  ground pepper
1 teaspoon sugar
2 tablespoons chopped
  fresh coriander

Heat the oil and fry the onion and garlic without browning. Add the tomatoes, chilies, salt, pepper, and sugar, and simmer for about 15 minutes, or until you have a thick purée. Add the coriander, remove from heat, and serve hot or cold.

🌶 **YIELD: 1 CUP**

〰〰 SHORTCUT MOLE SAUCE 〰〰

Use with turkey, chicken, or pork. *Mole* powder is available in Mexican specialty stores. See Turkey *Mole Poblano* (see pages 142–143) for a regular *mole poblano* sauce.

4 tablespoons peanut oil
2 medium onions, chopped
6 tomatoes, peeled and
  chopped (page 21)
2 cloves garlic, chopped

Heat the oil in a skillet and cook the onions until soft. Combine in an electric blender with the tomatoes and garlic. Add the *mole* powder, salt, and pepper and return to the skillet with

5 to 6 teaspoons *mole*
  powder
Coarse salt and freshly
  ground pepper
2 cups turkey or chicken
  stock
2 tablespoons sesame
  seeds

the stock. Simmer for 45 minutes. Sprinkle with sesame seeds. Heat the meat through in the sauce before serving.

🍂 **YIELD: 2 CUPS**

PEBRE

CHILEAN HOT SAUCE

Use this with meat and poultry. It is better than American bottled hot sauces and is used by Chileans in much the same way. It will keep for 1 or 2 weeks in a sealed jar.

1 tablespoon dried ground
  chilies (pages 13–16) or
  Red Chili Paste (page 30)
1 clove garlic, chopped
1 medium onion, chopped
1 bunch fresh coriander,
  chopped (parsley can be
  substituted)
1 tablespoon vinegar
2 tablespoons olive oil
½ cup water
Coarse salt to taste

Combine all the ingredients in a bowl, using the water to thin out the sauce. Leave for a couple of hours before using to develop the flavor.

🍂 **YIELD: ABOUT 1 CUP**

∿∿ MÔLHO DE PIMENTA E LIMÃO ∿∿

BRAZILIAN PEPPER AND LEMON SAUCE

Serve with *feijoada completa* or with pork sausages, corned beef, tongue, beef, or other cold meats.

4 bottled Tabasco peppers

1 medium onion, finely chopped

1 clove garlic, finely chopped

½ cup lemon juice

Coarse salt

Combine all the ingredients and keep overnight or a few hours to marinate before serving.

∿∿ PEANUT SATÉ SAUCE ∿∿

This goes particularly well with Chicken *Saté* (see page 141), for which it is the traditional accompaniment.

1 cup skinned roasted peanuts

2 tablespoons peanut oil

1 medium onion or ¼ cup shallots, chopped

1 clove garlic, chopped

1½ to 2 cups chicken stock

1 fresh red or green chili, minced (page 13–16)

1 to 1½ tablespoons soy sauce or *ketjap manis* (page 9)

1 tablespoon lime juice

Grind or blend the peanuts fine. Heat the oil in a skillet and fry the onion and the garlic without browning. Add the stock and bring to a boil. Add remaining ingredients and simmer for about 10 minutes. Thin out the sauce with more stock if necessary and serve hot.

❧ YIELD: 2 CUPS

〰〰 HOMEMADE MAYONNAISE 〰〰

This is so superior to bought mayonnaise that it is well worth the effort of making at home. All you need is a little patience. You can make mayonnaise in the blender but I find my method works, it takes very little time, and you can do the beating while you are watching the evening news.

Use about 4 yolks to a pint of oil. This will make about 2 cups. To lighten a mayonnaise add a little boiling water to it at the end.

1 egg yolk
Mustard
Olive oil
Lemon juice or vinegar
Coarse salt

I put the egg yolk in a bowl with a little mustard. I beat it until it becomes thick and sticky. Then I tilt the bowl and add a very little olive oil. Keeping the bowl tilted so that the oil stays in one side of the bowl and isn't directly on the egg, I gradually beat it into the egg until it is completely absorbed. I continue adding oil this way, adding a little more as the egg begins to absorb it more easily. I then add lemon juice or vinegar and salt and more oil until I have the right consistency.

NOTE: If it curdles I beat another egg yolk and add the curdled mixture to it bit by bit until it is smooth again. If your mixture curdles you have probably added too much oil too fast. Do not try to make mayonnaise on a very hot day.

⋁⋁⋏⋏ RED PEPPER SAUCE ⋁⋁⋏⋏

Serve this mild sauce with grilled meat, chicken, or fish. It is excellent with boiled or baked potatoes—instead of butter.

3 red bell peppers

3 shallots, coarsely chopped

1 clove garlic, coarsely chopped (green part removed)

½ teaspoon dried red chili flakes

2 to 3 tablespoons olive, walnut, or hazelnut oil

Coarse salt and freshly ground pepper to taste

2 to 3 tablespoons fresh tarragon leaves, chopped

Cut the peppers into eighths and place in a saucepan with the shallots, garlic, and chili flakes. Cover and cook over low heat until the peppers are soft (about 20 minutes). Place in the jar of a blender or food processor. Add the olive oil. Season with salt and pepper and blend until smooth. Correct seasoning and serve hot or cold. Just before serving, stir the tarragon into the sauce.

 **YIELD: ABOUT 1½ CUPS**

MARINADES

ORANGE-CHILI MARINADE
⋁⋀⋁ FOR PORK ⋁⋀⋁

This is very good for chops and roasts.

**1 cup freshly squeezed
  orange juice
2 tablespoons soy sauce
1 tablespoon chili powder
¼ cup olive oil
1 teaspoon thyme
Freshly ground pepper**

Combine ingredients and pour onto the meat and marinate, turning occasionally. Pork can be kept for 5 days in this mixture.

✿ YIELD: ENOUGH FOR A 5-POUND ROAST OR 6 CHOPS

YOGURT-CURRY MARINADE
⋁⋀⋁ FOR LAMB ⋁⋀⋁

Lamb chops and leg of lamb become more tender and get a crispy skin after being marinated in this mixture.

**1 cup yogurt
1 tablespoon Mild Curry
  Powder (page 26)
1 tablespoon coriander
  seeds**

Combine all ingredients. Coat the meat and let stand for up to a week. The longer you leave it, the better the lamb will be.

✿ YIELD: ENOUGH FOR A 5- TO 6-POUND ROAST OR 6 CHOPS

∿∿ YOGURT-PAPRIKA MARINADE ∿∿

This is for lamb or veal. Lamb keeps for up to a week, veal for a couple of days.

1 cup yogurt
**2 tablespoons Hungarian
  paprika**

Combine ingredients.

❧ **YIELD: ENOUGH FOR A 5- TO 6-POUND ROAST**

MUSTARD SEED–SOY SAUCE ∿∿ MARINADE FOR LAMB ∿∿

This is great for leg of lamb.

**2 tablespoons Dijon
  mustard**
**2 tablespoons mustard
  seed**
¼ cup soy sauce
¼ cup olive oil
**½ teaspoon rosemary
  (optional)**

Combine ingredients. Coat the leg of lamb with this dressing and marinate for up to a week.

❧ **YIELD: ENOUGH FOR A 4 POUND LEG OF LAMB.**

∿∿ CHERMOULA ∿∿

MOROCCAN MARINADE FOR FISH

This marinade can be made hotter with extra crushed chili peppers or cayenne pepper. Leave the fish to marinate for at least an hour so that the spices can penetrate it. The fish can then be baked in the oven or cooked on top of the stove.

1 cup fresh coriander leaves

4 cloves garlic, peeled

2 tablespoons vinegar

Juice of 1 lemon or lime

1 tablespoon paprika

1 tablespoon ground cumin

½ teaspoon crushed chilies (pages 13–16)

Cayenne and coarse salt to taste

2 tablespoons olive oil

Combine the ingredients in an electric blender and mix until smooth. For a better tasting marinade, work the coriander together with the garlic and vinegar with a mortar and pestle. Add the remaining ingredients and mix thoroughly.

❧ **YIELD: ENOUGH FOR 4 POUNDS OF FISH**

PEPPER-WINE MARINADE
∿∿ FOR STEAK ∿∿

This will make a tough steak tender. Cook the steak under low heat, first coating it with oil so that the juices will be sealed in. Slow cooking also helps to prevent toughening of meat—but this does not mean you need to overcook it.

1 tablespoon minced fresh ginger

1 clove garlic, minced

½ cup dry red wine

1 tablespoon dark mustard

1 tablespoon freshly ground black pepper

Combine all the ingredients and pour onto the steaks. Marinate overnight if possible, or at room temperature for a couple of hours. When ready to cook, remove the steaks from the marinade and dry them with paper towels. Coat them with oil and grill them. Meanwhile bring the marinade to a boil, and spoon resulting sauce over the steaks before serving.

❧ **YIELD: ENOUGH FOR 2 MEDIUM-SIZE STEAKS**

YOGURT–MUSTARD SEED
ᜊᜊᜊ MARINADE FOR LAMB ᜊᜊᜊ

Lamb can be refrigerated in this mixture for up to a week. When roasted medium-rare it comes out remarkably tender.

1 cup plain yogurt
1 teaspoon crushed
cardamom seed
½ teaspoon ground cumin
½ teaspoon ground
allspice
1 tablespoon mustard
seeds
¼ teaspoon ground mace
Coarse salt and freshly
ground pepper

Mix together all the ingredients and work into the lamb flesh. Turn the lamb occasionally in the mixture as it marinates. While it is roasting, pour a little oil onto the lamb.

❧ YIELD: ENOUGH FOR A 4- TO 6-POUND LEG OF LAMB

SENEGALESE MARINADE
ᜊᜊᜊ FOR MEAT, CHICKEN, OR FISH ᜊᜊᜊ

This is excellent for grilled meat or fish. Leave the meat in the mixture for several hours. Grill over high heat, turning frequently, and serve with rice.

4 to 5 lemons
1 medium onion, minced
2 green chilies, minced
(pages 14–16)
Coarse salt and freshly
ground pepper

Combine ingredients, pour onto meat, and toss thoroughly. Let stand for a few hours at room temperature before cooking.

❧ YIELD: ENOUGH FOR 1½ TO 2 POUNDS OF MEAT, CHICKEN, OR FISH

CHINESE HOISIN-CHILI
⌇⌇ MARINADE FOR PORK ⌇⌇

This marinade is good for roasts and chops. Serve the cooked meat with rice or Chinese vegetables.

Hoisin sauce is available in Chinese specialty shops and some supermarkets.

1 tablespoon *hoisin* sauce
1 tablespoon chili sauce
1-inch piece of fresh
  ginger, sliced
2 scallions, chopped
2 cloves garlic, chopped
¼ cup dry sherry
2 tablespoons soy sauce
1 tablespoon honey
Coarse salt
Freshly ground pepper

Combine all the ingredients and rub into the meat. Let stand overnight or for a couple of days. When cooking the meat, baste it with the marinade.

✿ **YIELD: ENOUGH FOR 3 TO 4 POUNDS MEAT.**

CHUTNEYS, PICKLES, RELISHES & CONDIMENTS

No Indian, Indonesian, or Mexican meal is complete without the traditional condiments. There is an astonishing diversity of chutneys and relishes in Indian and Pakistani cooking, ranging from mild and sweet to sharp and pungent in taste. Homemade chutneys are, of course, infinitely superior to store-bought ones and keep successfully in sealed jars away from the light. They improve over the months. I suggest that you make chutney in fairly large quantities at a time because you may be surprised at how fast it goes.

Indonesian cooking, which is a mixture of sweet, sour, and hot flavors, is always accompanied by a fiery *sambal*. Remember that these dishes are supposed to be eaten with plenty of rice and in fairly small quantities. You may find that on their own they are far too hot.

Mustard is an important Western condiment and variations on that theme are extensive. Homemade mustard is delicious and keeps well.

Various spicy butters are included in this chapter. They can be used with meats and fish and also to spread on canapés for a different flavor.

〰〰 MOROCCAN PRESERVED LEMONS 〰〰

These lemons are used in Moroccan *tajines* (stews). They have no substitute.

6 lemons
Coarse salt
3-inch cinnamon stick
5 coriander seeds, whole
5 peppercorns, whole
1 bay leaf
3 cloves, whole
Lemon juice, as necessary

Quarter the lemons, cutting down to within an inch of the bottom. Salt the pulp and reshape them. Put a layer of salt on the bottom of a glass pickling jar. Pack in the lemons, adding salt and remaining spices as you go. If the lemons are not covered by their own juice, squeeze more lemon juice on top. Let stand for 30 days, tightly covered, and turn every day.

To use, remove as much as needed and rinse under cold running water. The lemons will keep for up to a year.

 YIELD: 6 PRESERVED LEMONS

ᴡᴠᴠ GREEN MANGO CHUTNEY ᴡᴠᴠ

Green mangoes sometimes appear in the markets (they are always picked green for export) and they make an excellent chutney. This one is very easy to make and improves if it is left for several months before being used. It is a mild chutney and contains no chilies.

6 green mangoes

1 cup white wine vinegar

1 cup brown sugar

1 cup raisins

2-inch piece of fresh ginger

4 scallions

With a sharp knife cut the skin and meat from the mango seeds (because the mangoes are unripe, the flesh will not peel away easily). Discard the seeds and chop the mangoes into small pieces. Combine the vinegar, sugar, and raisins in a saucepan and bring to a boil. Meanwhile, peel and slice the ginger into thin strips and chop the scallions. Add the mangoes, scallions, and ginger to the vinegar mixture and simmer, covered, for about half an hour, or until thick. Pour into clean, warm, 1-pint glass pickling jars and seal tightly.

❧ **YIELD: ABOUT 4 CUPS**

NOTE: I suggest you make four times the amount of this recipe at once. If you don't, you may regret it later, not only because it is simpler to get the chutney making done all at one time, but green mangoes may not be for sale again for a while.

‿‿‿ TOMATO CHUTNEY ‿‿‿

This chutney is excellent with cold ham.

**2 pounds tomatoes,
   peeled and chopped
   (page 21)**
3 medium onions, chopped
1 cup vinegar
**3 fresh red chilies,
   chopped (pages 13–16)**
3 cloves garlic, minced
½ teaspoon ground cumin
1 3-inch cinnamon stick
Juice of half a lemon
**Coarse salt and freshly
   ground pepper**
½ cup sugar

Put the tomatoes in a saucepan with the remaining ingredients except sugar. Bring to a boil and add the sugar. Simmer for 10 to 15 minutes, until chutney begins to thicken. Cool and store in sterile glass pickling jars.

❧ **YIELD: ABOUT 4 CUPS**

CORIANDER AND COCONUT ‿‿‿ CHUTNEY ‿‿‿

Use fresh coriander only (available at Chinese, Latin American, and Indian grocers); do not substitute parsley. Once made, this will keep for a week.

1 bunch fresh coriander
**2 medium onions, coarsely
   chopped**
**1-inch piece of fresh
   ginger, coarsely
   chopped**

Trim the leaves from the coriander and put them in a blender with remaining ingredients. Blend and pour into a small bowl.

❧ **YIELD: 1½ CUPS**

1 fresh red or green chili
(pages 13–16)
½ coconut, coarsely
chopped
Juice of 1 lemon
¼ cup water
Coarse salt

LEMON AND MUSTARD SEED
〰〰 CHUTNEY 〰〰

This is a delicious chutney for fish or chicken. Limes may be used instead of the lemons.

6 large lemons
4 medium onions
Coarse salt
2 cups white wine vinegar
4 tablespoons mustard
seed
1 teaspoon ground
allspice
1 pound light brown sugar
¼ pound raisins

Slice the lemons (with peel) thinly, and peel and slice the onions. Place all on a large board or plate and sprinkle with salt. Let stand for a day.

Put the lemons and onions into a large heavy-bottomed saucepan with the remaining ingredients. Cover and simmer for about 45 minutes over low heat. Pour into warm, clean, glass pickling jars and seal.

🌿 YIELD: 3 CUPS

∿∿ INDIAN LIME PICKLE ∿∿

12 limes
Coarse salt
3 green chilies (pages 14–16)
4 tablespoons green ginger, chopped
Juice of 3 to 4 limes
1 bay leaf

Quarter the limes and remove the seeds. Salt the bottom of a glass pickling jar and arrange a layer of the limes, with any juices that may have run from them, adding a few chilies and pieces of ginger. Salt. Repeat until jar is full, then pour in lime juice and add bay leaf. Shake thoroughly. Let stand, tightly closed, for 30 days, turning once a day. This will keep for up to a year.

❧ **YIELD: 1 QUART**

CHILI, ONION, ∿∿ AND TOMATO SAMBAL ∿∿

The following *sambals* are traditional Indonesian condiments, all containing hot chilies. They are served in small bowls to accompany *satés*, and as relishes with Indonesian meals.

This chili, onion, and tomato *sambal* goes particularly well with beef, pork, or chicken *satés*, and with grilled or barbecued meats.

1 tomato, diced
1 medium onion, diced
1 fresh red chili, diced
1 green chili, diced (pages 14–16)
¼ cup fresh lime juice

Combine the ingredients in a small bowl and allow to marinate together for a couple of hours at room temperature before using.

❧ **YIELD: ABOUT ¾ CUP**

∿∿ HARISSA SAUCE ∿∿

MOROCCAN HOT RELISH

This relish is particularly good with black or green olives. Toss the olives in the mixture and serve as an hors d'oeuvre. You can buy canned *harissa* paste in specialty food stores.

4 dried red chili peppers (pages 13–14)
2 cloves garlic, peeled
1 tablespoon caraway seeds
1 teaspoon ground cumin
1 teaspoon ground coriander seed
Coarse salt
Olive oil

Soak the peppers for an hour, drain them, and cut them small. In a mortar pound them with the garlic, caraway seeds, cumin, coriander, and salt. Put the mixture in a jar and cover with a layer of olive oil. It will keep for 2 to 3 months in a refrigerator.

 **YIELD: ½ CUP**

∿∿ SAMBAL KETJAP ∿∿

Use this Indonesian hot sauce with *saté* dishes, kabobs, and barbecued meats. If you cannot find *ketjap* in local specialty stores, use soy sauce instead.

1 cup *ketjap*
⅓ cup fresh lime juice
2 fresh green chilies (pages 14–16)

Combine *ketjap* and fresh lime juice. Finely chop chilies and mix in. Serve in a small bowl.

 **YIELD: 1½ CUPS**

ᐯᐯᐯᐯ APPLE AND MINT SAMBAL ᐯᐯᐯᐯ

Serve in a separate bowl with Indonesian dishes; curries; and grilled or barbecued meat, fish, or poultry.

2 raw apples
Small bunch fresh mint
4 green chilies (pages 14–16)
Juice of 1 lemon or lime
Coarse salt to taste

Finely chop apples (with peel), mint, and chilies and moisten with the juice of a lemon or lime. Season with coarse salt. This will keep, refrigerated, for a couple of days.

 **YIELD: 1 CUP**

ᐯᐯᐯᐯ INDONESIAN CUCUMBER RELISH ᐯᐯᐯᐯ

This is good with Oriental dishes, grilled meat, and *satés*. It will keep refrigerated for a couple of weeks.

3 tablespoons sesame or peanut oil
1 medium onion, chopped
1 clove garlic, chopped
½ teaspoon crushed chili peppers
¼ teaspoon cayenne pepper
½ teaspoon turmeric
½ teaspoon ground cumin seed
Coarse salt to taste
2 cucumbers, peeled and diced

Heat the oil in a skillet and soften the onion with the garlic. Add remaining ingredients (except cucumbers) and cook for 10 minutes. Pour over the cucumbers and cool. Let stand overnight, if possible, before using.

 **YIELD: 1 CUP**

⌁⌁ INDONESIAN HOT PEPPER RELISH ⌁⌁

Use with Indonesian dishes, curries, barbecued lamb, or fish. Serve it in a small bowl.

1 cup grated coconut
2 fresh red chili peppers
(pages 13–16)
1 medium onion, chopped
Juice of 1 lemon or lime

In a blender combine all ingredients. A pestle and mortar may be used in place of the blender.

❧ YIELD: 1¼ CUPS

⌁⌁ HERB MUSTARD ⌁⌁

You can buy this mustard ready-made, but it is even better made at home. Use it with cold fish (especially salmon), chicken, beef, or ham. It has a lovely deep green color.

1 cup Dijon mustard
2 tablespoons fresh basil,
chopped
2 tablespoons fresh
parsley, chopped
2 tablespoons fresh
tarragon, chopped
2 tablespoons fresh
chives, chopped

In a blender combine all ingredients and blend until fine. Keep refrigerated in a tightly sealed jar.

❧ YIELD: 1 CUP

⋎⋏⋎ PICKLED MUSTARD ⋎⋏⋎

Use with cold fish, chicken, stuffed eggs, beef, or sandwiches.

1 cup Dijon mustard
2 tablespoons capers, chopped
2 tablespoons sweet pickles, chopped
2 tablespoons dill pickles
2 tablespoons dry white wine or beer

Combine mustard with capers, sweet pickles, and dill pickles. Moisten with dry white wine or beer. Keep in a tightly sealed jar in the refrigerator.

❧ **YIELD: 1½ CUPS**

⋎⋏⋎ SPICED MUSTARD ⋎⋏⋎

2 large onions, chopped
2 cloves garlic, chopped
2 cups red wine vinegar
1 cup dry mustard
2 tablespoons coarsely ground mustard seed
½ teaspoon cayenne
2 teaspoons coarse salt
Mustard oil

Marinate the onions and garlic in the vinegar overnight. Strain the marinade and reserve. Combine the remaining ingredients (except mustard oil) in a bowl and mix with 1½ cups of the marinade. Pour the rest of the marinade into a saucepan. Bring to a boil and stir in the mustard paste. Simmer for 5 minutes. Cool. Stir in enough mustard oil to make a smooth paste. Pour into crocks or jars and cover tightly. Store in a cool place.

❧ **YIELD: 1½ CUPS**

〜〜 CHINESE MUSTARD 〜〜

The Chinese make their mustard fresh before each meal because once made, if left for a long time, it loses flavor. Serve this in a small bowl with Chinese dishes. It is also good with beef.

Beer can be used instead of water (a good way to use up flat beer).

½ cup dry Chinese or English mustard
Boiling water

Put the mustard in a small bowl and add the water until you have a smooth and rather runny paste. Leave for half an hour or so before using so that the mustard has time to develop its flavor.

🌿 YIELD: ½ CUP

〜〜 DANISH MUSTARD 〜〜

Use this on Danish open-face sandwiches, with herring, salmon, eggs, or beef. It is a hot mustard.

½ cup dry mustard
6 tablespoons light brown sugar
¼ cup boiling water
3 to 4 tablespoons peanut or vegetable oil
2 teaspoons Worcestershire sauce
1 teaspoon white wine or cider vinegar

Combine mustard with sugar and add boiling water to make a paste. Beat in Worcestershire sauce and wine. Set aside for an hour before using so that the flavor has time to develop.

🌿 YIELD: 1 CUP

⌁⌁ DEVILED BUTTER ⌁⌁

1 stick softened unsalted
  butter
1 tablespoon Tabasco
  sauce
2 tablespoons
  Worcestershire sauce
1 teaspoon dry mustard
1 tablespoon minced
  onion or shallot
1 tablespoon chopped
  chives
1 tablespoon chopped
  parsley
Coarse salt and freshly
  ground pepper

Mash the butter in a bowl and work
in the remaining ingredients. Form
into an oblong shape and refrigerate.
Slice to serve.

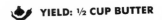 **YIELD:** ½ CUP BUTTER

⌁⌁ MUSTARD BUTTER ⌁⌁

Serve with ham, beef, or fish.

1 stick softened unsalted
  butter
2 tablespoons Dijon
  mustard
Cayenne to taste

Combine butter with mustard. Add a
little cayenne and shape into a ball or
smooth out the mixture in a small
bowl. Refrigerate for an hour before
using.

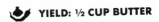 **YIELD:** ½ CUP BUTTER

ᐯᐯᐯ **BEURRE À L'INDIENNE** ᐯᐯᐯ

Use with chicken, lamb, or ham. It can also be used on grilled kidneys or as a spread for sandwiches or toast.

1 stick softened unsalted
butter

1 teaspoon Mild Curry
Powder (page 26)

1 teaspoon dry mustard

1 tablespoon mango
chutney, chopped

Dash Worcestershire sauce

Dash Tabasco sauce

Lemon juice to taste

Coarse salt and freshly
ground pepper

Combine all ingredients, seasoning to taste. Use at room temperature for spreading on bread. To serve with meat, shape into a cylinder or smooth out in a small bowl and refrigerate for an hour or until ready to use.

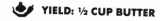 **YIELD: ½ CUP BUTTER**

ᾱᾱ **PAPRIKA BUTTER** ᾱᾱ

Use good Hungarian paprika or this will have no taste. It goes with grilled chicken, veal, or fish.

½ onion, minced
Butter for frying
1 tablespoon Hungarian
  paprika
1 stick softened unsalted
  butter

Sauté onion in a little butter. Add paprika and combine in a bowl with stick of butter. Sieve the mixture and refrigerate until ready to use.

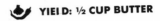 **YIELD: ½ CUP BUTTER**

INDEX

〰〰